Nature's
Blessings

Nature's Blessings

CONNECT WITH THE EARTH EVERY DAY THROUGH SIMPLE ACTIVITIES, MANTRAS, AND MEDITATIONS

Kirsten Riddle

CICO BOOKS

LONDON NEW YORK

Acknowledgments

I would like to thank Carmel Edmonds and the
wonderful team at CICO for all their work on
creating this special book.

Published in 2022 by CICO Books
An imprint of Ryland Peters & Small Ltd
20–21 Jockey's Fields   341 E 116th St
London WC1R 4BW   New York, NY 10029

www.rylandpeters.com

10 9 8 7 6 5 4 3 2 1

Text © Alison Davies 2022
Design and illustration © CICO Books 2022

A CIP catalog record for this book is available from the
Library of Congress and the British Library.

ISBN: 978-1-80065-159-3

Printed in China

Editor: Karen Rigden
Illustrator: Michael Hill

Commissioning editor: Kristine Pidkameny
Senior designer: Emily Breen
Art director: Sally Powell
Creative director: Leslie Harrington
Production manager: Gordana Simakovic
Publishing manager: Carmel Edmonds

MIX
Paper | Supporting
responsible forestry
FSC
www.fsc.org   FSC® C008047

Contents

Introduction

Nature nurtures. It ebbs and flows and moves in a timeless dance that impacts upon our surroundings, but it is more than just something to witness. The water that flows from the heavens, streaming into the lakes and rivers, fills your cup. The earth you stand upon is more than just a platform, it is a teeming bed of life from which crops and flowers grow. Rooted saplings become shrubs and then trees which stand tall and proud, as they filter pollutants and purify the air you breathe. It is a constantly evolving greenhouse which sustains all manner of life.

It's no wonder that experiencing the magic of nature is a "pick me up" for the soul. Stepping out of the gray and into the green of wide-open spaces is a tonic which reduces stress, lifts the spirits, and even eases depression. Breathing fresh air and taking in the beauty of the landscape soothe a fractious mind, for when you take the time to seek out those pockets of peace and enjoy the elements, you make every day special.

A sacred life is there for the taking if we engage with the environment and learn from it. There is so much wisdom to be gained from a stroll in the countryside, or a moment spent watching the birds in the garden. Luckily for us, nature is a patient teacher, always present and willing to show the way if you make the time to reconnect. Our ancestors knew this too. Without the trappings of technology, they led a simple, unsheltered life that allowed them to spend time beneath the stars, gazing up at their beauty, to marvel at the movement of the sun and the constantly shifting phases of the moon, and to watch the animals hunting and gathering. They worked with the changing rhythms of the earth to survive and thrive. The relationship between humans and the natural world was key to everything.

The Native Americans have long believed that everything has a spirit, a life force that we can see and feel, and they weren't the only ones. The Celts, too, held this belief. They thought that every tree, plant, and stone had an energy that could be harnessed. Ancient peoples from around the globe worshipped the power of nature and gave thanks for its gifts. They realized that they could work with it and channel the unique wisdom of each of its blessings to bring balance, stability, strength, and renewal.

In today's world it can be hard to connect with the landscape in the same way. If you live in the city, the natural world seems so far away—but this book shows you how to engage with the environment and make the most of nature's blessings wherever you are right now. Whether you live in an urban jungle or a rural town, in the suburbs or on an island, you can experience the natural world at a deeper level, using a little imagination and some fun tips and tricks. You can shift your perspective and tap into the creative power of the earth to enhance your life and bring about positive change.

Divided into four easy-to-read sections which represent the elements, Air, Earth, Fire, and Water, this book offers a selection of nature's blessings. All you have to do is pick the element, then the creature or natural creation you're drawn to, and discover how you can harness its specific energy throughout your day. From birds and bees, to flowers and trees, the sun in the sky, and the moon and the breeze, there's an array of options to match your mood and lift the spirits. There are exercises and rituals to show how you can set an intention at different stages of your day and connect with the inherent power of your chosen element. Throughout the sections you'll find highlighted themes, ideas, and positive lessons that make it easy for you to tap into the wonder and force of the natural world. Each entry provides a fascinating insight into folklore and includes a final meditation and a journaling section to help you wind down and reflect.

Whether you're feeling vulnerable and need strength and grounding, or you're trying to be more intuitive in your decision making, this book will help you find what you're looking for. Each chapter has an introduction that highlights all the key themes covered. Dip in and explore, or pick a blessing a day and make it a part of your routine. Once you get into the habit of setting an intention, and performing rituals and mindful techniques, you can create your own by choosing things in nature that you find fascinating and learning more about them. All you need is an open heart and mind and a willingness to reconnect. Nature's blessings are in abundance at any time of the year, and they are here for you to experience.

CHAPTER 1

The Element of Air

Air

Air invigorates. It sweeps away the debris and clears a path for something new. Without it, we would not survive, but it is so much more than oxygen. It has the power to transform a landscape. The bristling, bustling thrill of the wind as it whips through your hair, the gentle kiss of a breeze upon the cheek. The way it wraps around your body, propelling you forward in directions that you could never expect. Air is a game changer. It refreshes and energizes all it meets.

The element of Air is all about rejuvenation and creativity. It governs the space above your head and, as such, is associated with intellect and the generation of new ideas. Being in the air gives a sense of freedom. When we take flight, our perspective shifts and we're able to see the bigger picture. The world becomes much larger and we realize the wealth of opportunity at our feet. The creatures that live most of their life in the air appreciate this; they have an openness that carries them through each day.

Within this section you will find an array of nature's blessings associated with the air, from the rainbow that bursts with color in the sky, to the birds that skim the treetops in search of a lofty roost. All the many airborne creatures that inhabit your environment and the breeze itself have the power to manifest change. You'll learn how tapping into their energy can stimulate the mind and activate your imagination. You'll discover your inventive side and also give your energy levels and immunity a boost. Take a deep breath in, fill your lungs, then exhale and let the pages fall open.

AIR ACTIVITIES

To help you connect with this element, try to incorporate some of these activities into your schedule.

- Stand on the top of a high space—such as a building, bridge, hill, or even mountain—and breathe in the clean air
- Go for a walk on a windy day
- Open your windows and let the breeze blow through
- Fly a kite
- Ride in a convertible car with the roof down, or ride a bike downhill
- Lie beneath the stars
- Stand among the trees on a breezy day and listen to the leaves rustling
- Breathe, long and deep

Blackbird

Awareness • Ideas • Joy • Spontaneity

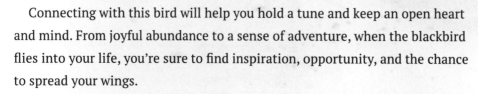

The cheerful blackbird is a generous performer and
wastes no time in unleashing its song upon the world.
It's as if this charming creature knows the effect it
has on those who are blessed enough to hear it. A sure
sign that spring has sprung, the blackbird is a welcome
visitor to any garden and can be encouraged to come again with seeds
and a well-mown lawn.

Connecting with this bird will help you hold a tune and keep an open heart
and mind. From joyful abundance to a sense of adventure, when the blackbird
flies into your life, you're sure to find inspiration, opportunity, and the chance
to spread your wings.

Your daily intention

*"Today I shall be like a joyful blackbird in flight; I will sing my song with
pride and let the melody lift me higher."*

Follow this ritual to promote happiness, inspired by the blackbird's delightful song.

1 Sit on the edge of your bed, place your feet firmly on the floor and your hands on
   your stomach, just above the belly button.

2 Breathe in deeply and as you exhale open your mouth and let out an "ahhh" noise.

3 Feel the sound reverberating through your chest and throat, and keep it going for
   as long as possible.

4 Repeat the mantra, thinking about the note you just produced, and try repeating the note one more time: "Today I shall be like a joyful blackbird in flight; I will sing my song with pride and let the melody lift me higher."

5 Feel the energy of your song infusing you with joy for the day ahead.

Blackbird folklore

Often linked to magic and mystery, the blackbird was considered sacred by the Druids, who believed it was a messenger from the spirit world. The dark, iridescent feathers appear to shift shape and form in the light, so it's no surprise that this gentle bird is also a friend to those who practice shamanism. It's thought the blackbird's song can transport you to other realms if you listen carefully.

According to the Native American folklore of the Plains tribes, when blackbirds ate the crops, it was a bad omen and a sign that the tribe had done something wrong. For those who want to practice the magical arts, this joyous bird is a powerful totem and a symbol of mystery and the unknown. If witchcraft isn't your thing, the blackbird can help you reflect and discover your true purpose.

Folklore fix

Keep a picture of a blackbird by your side when you meditate. Bring the image to mind and let the bird take you on a magical journey.

Every day is a new adventure to be enjoyed.

Awareness: Listen and engage

From the flutter of tiny wings to the gentle sing-song melody of its call, the blackbird is a joy to behold, but how many times do you really listen to the birds? Make a point of stopping during your day and let nature's symphony inspire you. Close your eyes and listen to the world around you. Take in the background noise and try to pick out the sounds one by one. You might be surprised at some of the things you notice. Noise tends to blend into one, but when we really listen, we're able to identify all the notes that make up the general tune. Finally, listen to your breathing. Focus on the sound and the rise and fall of your chest.

Spontaneity: Spread the joy

A simple bird-feeding ritual can help you connect with blackbird's vibrant energy. All you need are some old pieces of bread and a little time.

1 Break the bread into tiny pieces and crumbs in a bowl.

2 Find a spot outside. This could be in your backyard or local park—anywhere that there is easily accessible green space. Spin around and scatter the bread in all directions.

3 As you spin, embrace the air element. Feel the breeze on your face and enjoy the sense of freedom this brings.

4 Make a silent wish to the blackbird to bless you with abundance and joy.

Joy: Find your song

The blackbird's theme tune is its beautiful song, but what's yours? For a quick pick-me-up, think of a song that instantly gets your feet tapping and makes you want to dance. Bring it to mind and sing along in your head. Whatever you're doing—walking, typing, cooking, cleaning—do it to the beat of your own theme tune and you'll feel instantly brighter.

Ideas: Let your creativity fly

Use the intricate pattern of a bird's feather to bring out your creative side. Find a picture of a feather, and either have a go at sketching it or, if you prefer, write a few sentences describing what you see. Think of what the feather represents and how it makes you feel, then draw or write from the heart.

Let yourself go and see where the feather takes you. You might end up drawing the entire bird or making a collage of feather shapes. If you're writing, you could end up with a poem, a story, or just a few sentences that bring the image to life. The important thing is to let your imagination fly free and create something personal to you.

MEDITATION

Find a quiet spot and let the beauty of the blackbird lift you up.

Imagine you're sitting in a beautiful garden. It's a glorious summer's day and the sun is shining. A blackbird lands at your feet. Its bright eyes hold your gaze and you are mesmerized. You watch as the bird moves closer, glossy black wings brushing the fresh grass. It chirps a cheery greeting, then in a moment it is gone, up in the air in a flurry of wings. You watch as it takes to the sky, soaring high among the fluffy white clouds. For a minute, you wish you too could fly. You imagine what it would be like to rise from the ground, to be limitless and free. You take a deep breath in and feel the air filling your lungs, and as you exhale, you release all of the day's tension. You continue to breathe deeply, to release the weight of your worries until you feel that you too could fly away.

Journaling inspiration

- Consider what brought you joy today. Single out those moments that made you smile, and write them down. Give thanks for each one.

- Think of the ways that you made others smile today, and how you can bring more joy into the world.

Butterfly

**Metamorphosis • Restoration
Freedom • Gentleness**

The gentle touch of a butterfly wing is like a whisper from the heavens, full of joy and potential. This delicate creature has a lightness of being, and a way of bringing sunshine to each moment. When it alights on a flower to soak up the sun, it brings a moment of respite. Butterflies symbolize transformation, the idea that we can move from one state to another and reinvent ourselves.

Working with the energy of this creature can help you understand the process of renewal at work in your own life. You'll feel the lightness of letting go, of spending valuable moments of stillness beneath the sun's energizing rays and appreciating the joy that each new day brings.

Your daily intention

"Today I will be like a butterfly basking in the midday sun; I will dance from flower to flower, with joy and lightness."

Set your daily intention with this butterfly-inspired exercise.

1 Lie on the floor and focus on the rise and fall of your chest.

2 Take a deep breath in, and notice how your diaphragm moves, then release the breath slowly.

3 Repeat, several times, until you feel totally relaxed.

4 Imagine you're resting on a flower head. Steadily stretch your arms and legs out at the sides, to make a star shape, like a butterfly extending its wings.

5 Repeat your morning mantra with feeling: "Today I will be like a butterfly basking in the midday sun; I will dance from flower to flower, with joy and lightness."

Butterfly folklore

The simple act of transformation, as the humble caterpillar blossoms into the butterfly, is a miracle of nature, and something the ancients valued. To them, this tiny creature showed innate strength, resilience, and the ability to be reborn. As such the butterfly became an emblem of hope and joy in many cultures.

The Chinese associated it with love in its purest form, and love letters were often signed with a butterfly sigil. In Japanese culture it was thought that white butterflies were the souls of lost loved ones. The Romans believed they were a symbol of marriage, and butterfly images were etched into coins. The Native Americans, meanwhile, saw them as spiritual messengers, able to carry their wishes to the gods.

A universal symbol of resurrection, the butterfly is a popular totem, thought to attract love and happiness.

Gentleness: Sense and touch

Stop and consider how you feel right now. Are you happy, sad, stressed? Now turn your attention to the physical world. What can you feel right now? Can you sense the air around you? Can you feel the ground cushion each foot? What about your face; can you sense the breeze grazing your cheek, or the sun's warmth on your forehead?

Folklore fix

Treat yourself to a bunch of your favorite blooms, arrange them in a vase, and appreciate their beauty, just as a butterfly would. Write a wish for happiness on a piece of paper and place it beneath the vase.

Focus on the gentleness of nature. Sometimes you have to really concentrate to notice what is going on around you, to pick out those feelings that you might normally take for granted.

You are a part of the environment; you impact your surroundings and vice versa. The gentlest of touches can make all the difference, by helping you see the wonder all around you. To finish, consider your emotions right now. Have they changed from when you started this exercise?

Restoration: Take a shower of light

When a butterfly needs to recharge, it takes some time to rest. It spreads its glorious wings and absorbs the warmth of the sun. Even on the darkest of days, you can renew your spirit by standing in a shower of light and giving your aura, the body's energy field, a boost of brightness.

For this exercise, find a quiet spot where you won't be disturbed—a five-minute bathroom break will do.

1 Stand with your feet hip-width apart, tilt your chin upward, and lengthen your spine.

2 Each time you breathe in, feel your chest expand.

3 Imagine a shower of golden light coming down from the heavens. It hits the top of your head, your chest, your belly, and cascades down your body. It covers every part of you and is also absorbed into your skin. It fills your chest and stomach. It flows to all your limbs, to your fingers and toes. It shimmers with cleansing energy, which restores every part of your being.

I am a radiant being,
filled with light and love.

MEDITATION

This magical meditation will soothe and lift your spirits.

You are sitting in the middle of a meadow filled with wildflowers. It is spring and the air is fresh and sweet. The lush green grass is damp with dew but soft to the touch. You lie back, the ground caresses you, and you feel the prickle of tiny leaf-blades against your skin. Above you a butterfly hovers, its fragile wings splayed against the backdrop of the sun. It lands on your chest, resting against your heart. You know it's there, but you hardly feel it, it is so delicate. You take a deep breath and feel the soothing energy of the butterfly imbue you with lightness. After a moment, it lifts its wings, circles your head one final time, and flies away, leaving you to marvel at the magic of nature.

Freedom: Flutter by

Butterflies flutter. They dance through the air with the grace of a prima ballerina. When you're looking to express yourself freely, take a moment to do something completely different. Get up and shake your body. Spin around and imagine you're floating through the air like a magical butterfly. Enjoy the freedom of moving your body and getting lost in the dance. A couple of minutes of activity will revive your imagination.

Metamorphosis: Mandala magic

Butterflies emerge from the chrysalis, reborn and ready to take center stage in the world. With symmetrical wings daubed in eye-catching patterns, there is nothing more striking or symbolic. A butterfly-inspired mandala can help you embrace the positive power of change and transform any part of your life.

Using a pencil, make a dot in the center of a piece of paper, then continue to create a series of circles around it, using more dots. You can connect the dots and make patterns working from the central point outward. Keep in mind the patterns you might see on a butterfly, or use a picture as inspiration. As you draw, ponder the nature of transformation. Imagine that you are in the chrysalis state, poised to emerge and show the world the "real" you. What would you like the world to see? Think of patterns and colors you might use to represent this moment of change, and incorporate them into your design. Most importantly, have fun! When you've finished, position the mandala somewhere that you'll see it every day.

Journaling inspiration

- Reflect on your day and write about any moments when you felt uplifted. If you can't find any, consider why, and what was dragging you down. How could you have seen the lighter side of things? Maybe you could have been gentler with yourself and others?

- Write down some suggestions to help lift you up as you go about your day.

Wind

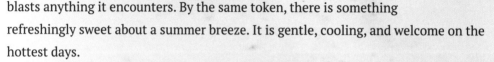

**Purification • Potential
Change • Drive**

Untamed and feral, the wind is not a force that
can be controlled. If you're caught in the middle
of a blustery breeze, you cannot avoid it. There is
nothing that can stop the flow of air as it batters and
blasts anything it encounters. By the same token, there is something
refreshingly sweet about a summer breeze. It is gentle, cooling, and welcome on the
hottest days.

The wind is a force of nature, but one that can work in your favor when you face it
with an open heart. It clears the path for something new, sweeping through your life,
bringing change and the opportunity to grow. It bristles with potential, whips the
imagination into a frenzy, and offers the promise of excitement. When you harness
the power of the wind, you can make great strides toward personal fulfilment.

Your daily intention

*"Today I will embrace the wind as it blows through my world; I will
let it sweep away negative energy, and bring a blast of inspiration and
opportunity to my door."*

Use the morning mantra with the following exercise to set your intention for the day.

1 Close your eyes and imagine you're standing in an open field.

2 A sudden gust of wind wraps around you. It blows through every pore, tousling
your hair and taking your breath away. It clears away obstacles and removes any
bad thoughts that you have collected so far. It sweeps through your body and mind,
giving you a clean slate for the day.

3 Say the mantra at the top of your voice. Imagine you're shouting it into the wind: "Today I will embrace the wind as it blows through my world; I will let it sweep away negative energy, and bring a blast of inspiration and opportunity to my door."

Wind folklore

Invisible to the eye but able to make its presence felt, the wind can be seen as a changeable force, a celestial entity sent by the gods to deliver justice and blessings.

In some ancient traditions the wind was the messenger, a symbol of divine power and strength. The Japanese believed that the deity Raijin sent terrible winds, in the form of typhoons, to destroy his enemies. Known as Kamikaze, these gales wreaked havoc upon the earth and must have seemed like heavenly retribution.

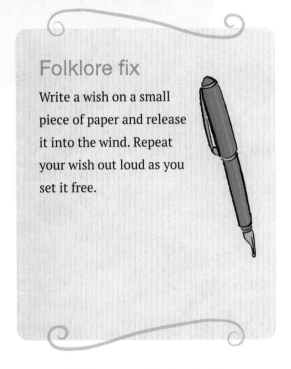

Folklore fix

Write a wish on a small piece of paper and release it into the wind. Repeat your wish out loud as you set it free.

The ancient Greeks collectively named the four directional winds Anemoi and believed them to be winged men, who could transform into gusts of air at will. The god Aeolus was the Keeper of the Winds, a lesser deity who could unleash the winds only with the say-so of more powerful gods.

Thought to represent the spirit world and the flow of life upon earth, the wind is also a powerful symbol in dreams, and an omen of change to come.

Potential: Breathe in your potential

Take a moment in your day to really feel the atmosphere that surrounds you. Stop what you're doing and stand in the flow of the air. Notice how it feels against your skin. Is it strong, or gentle? Brisk or smooth? Consider how it smells and tastes. Draw it into your lungs and notice how you feel as you gulp it down. For every breath there is more life and a sense of anticipation. The air propels you forward, and without it, there would be nothing. It is a part of you, and as such, each new breath is full of potential. Acknowledge this and make each portion of air count. Take longer, deeper breaths. Give thanks for each moment and consider how you can make every minute of your day count.

Drive: Be a whirlwind of ideas

Stimulate the imagination and generate new ideas with this exercise.

1 Bring your attention to the top of your head. Imagine a tiny whirling circle of energy in the center of your scalp. This spot is your crown chakra, the energy center which fires your imagination and stimulates your sixth sense.

2 Every time you exhale, the circle gets bigger, spinning like a mini whirlwind above your head. It extends upward and outward into a funnel shape, to catch thoughts and ideas. It acts as a conduit between your conscious and subconscious, allowing inspiration to flow into your brain and helping to motivate you.

3 See the whirlwind extend outward even more, until it almost fills all of the space above your head.

4 Close your eyes and let any thoughts come. Let them spiral down the tornado until they float into your mind, giving you the drive you need to act.

5 Give yourself a couple of minutes, then open your eyes and record any ideas or impressions that you have.

Purification: Clear stagnant energy

Imagine you're facing into the wind. It moves toward you as a sheet of air that is visible to the eye. It sparkles with light and fizzes with energy. Take a deep breath in and let the air wash over you. Draw it into your chest, then, as you exhale, release all the things that are holding you back.

MEDITATION

Lighten the load with this liberating visualization to help you relax.

Picture yourself standing at the edge of a cliff. There's a mist rising to greet the clouds, but you're aware of the ground dropping away beneath you. This is an isolated place, a space where you can be alone and drink in the beauty of nature. You can feel the wind nipping at your heels, gently nudging you closer to the edge. You take a breath and take a step into the unknown. A strong breeze scoops you up, and you find that you're hovering in mid-air, floating like a leaf in flight. Your body feels weightless and you drift gracefully, dipping and swaying. At last you are free, able to go with the flow and let the wind carry you where you need to be.

Change: Sow the seeds

Put a selection of bird seeds and nuts in a bowl and mix together. Imagine that every tiny seed is a seed of inspiration and has the potential to change your life. Take the bowl outside into the garden, scoop up a handful of the mixture you've prepared, and release it into the wind.

Continue to do this, creating patterns on the ground as you go; you might want to spin around as you do so. Have fun with this and imagine that with every design you create you're inviting change into your life, in whatever shape or form this may take. The patterns you've created continue to evolve as the wind blows the seed into new forms, just as life continues to flow and change. Every moment offers the opportunity for us to create a new future.

*I embrace change and open my heart
and mind to new opportunities.*

Journaling inspiration

- Spend time reflecting on your day. What would you go back and change if you could, and why? Write these thoughts down.

- Think about positive changes you can implement that would make each day easier.

- Think about even bigger changes you can make to help your life flow.

Owl

**Wisdom • Instinct
Empowerment • Stillness**

Gaze into the eyes of the owl and you will see everything
you need to know about the past, present, and future.
You will feel a sense of calm wash over you. This silent,
winged assassin is a creature of the night, able to blend
seamlessly into the environment. The enigmatic owl has
mystical associations all over the globe. With exceptional
hearing and the ability to see in the dark, embracing the
spirit of the owl is all about perception and using the gifts
you have been given, including your intuition, to read deeper meaning in everything
around you.

Harnessing owl energy will help you connect with your higher self and experience
the world on many different levels. You'll discover your true purpose in life, and how
you can use your unique gifts to fly higher and faster than ever before.

Your daily intention

*"Today I will be like the owl; I will draw on my innate wisdom and see
beyond the veil, to find my true calling."*

Use the morning mantra to set your intention and fire up your intuitive senses.

1 From a standing position, let your feet rock forward so that you're on your toes.

2 Take a breath and bring your arms up and out, in a swooping motion. Feel the
stretch in your spine and the back of your legs.

3 Exhale, roll back onto your heels, and crouch down, as if you're an owl landing
on a branch.

4 Take another deep breath and draw your body upward and back into the standing position.

5 Say your morning mantra to finish: "Today I will be like the owl; I will draw on my innate wisdom and see beyond the veil, to find my true calling."

Owl folklore

Magic and mystery are the realm of the owl. Known as the keeper of souls, and the guardian of the underworld in many ancient cultures, including the Egyptians and the Celts, the owl was revered. Thought to accompany the souls of the dead on their journey into the otherworld, the owl offered protection and strength beneath the cover of its wings.

To the ancient Greeks, the owl was a fortuitous symbol, associated with the goddess Athena, and as such represented wisdom, learning, and good fortune. The Native Americans believed that owls held sacred knowledge, because they seemed to predict weather conditions with their flight and could also see in the dark. In Europe, during the Middle Ages, owls were synonymous with witchcraft and thought to be witches in disguise.

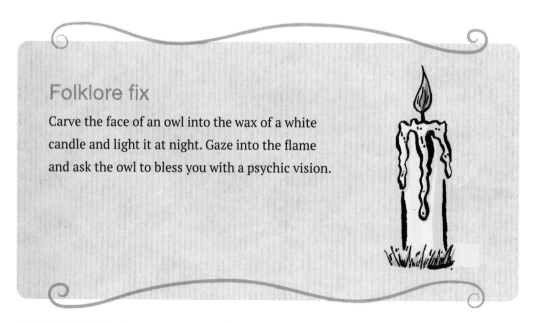

Folklore fix

Carve the face of an owl into the wax of a white candle and light it at night. Gaze into the flame and ask the owl to bless you with a psychic vision.

MEDITATION

Let the presence of the owl soothe away stress and fear with this visualization.

You stand beneath a veil of stars. The sky is a velvet blanket of darkness. You hold out your arm in front of you, and within seconds your feathered friend the owl is there, sitting on your wrist. Bright eyes that glisten like jewels look into your own, and you feel safe and loved. As your gaze locks deeper, you sense a soul connection which brings you strength and comfort. The owl speaks into your mind. It whispers words of wisdom and power. You let these mutterings settle and soothe your heart. You know that the owl will always be there, to bless you with its presence whenever you need it.

Stillness: Freeze the moment

Be still, just for a moment. This means you must stop everything you are doing right now. Do not move, do not fidget, do not let your mind run away with you. Still your thoughts and fears. Imagine that time has frozen and you are caught in its grip. All you can do is breathe and be in the moment. Don't beat yourself up if you can't hold on to the stillness. Just focus on the rise and fall of your chest as you breathe.

Notice the rhythmic pattern of each breath and slow it right down. Extend both your inward and outward breath. Practice being still for one minute, then, when you feel confident, increase this by 30 seconds at a time. Finding stillness can help you deal with stress. You'll be able to call on this power when you're feeling overwhelmed, and it will calm your body and mind.

I have all the answers I need within me.

Empowerment: Cloak yourself in power

An owl's outer feathers have special comb-like serrations on the edges
which allow them to fly almost soundlessly through the night sky, while the
larger feathers on their wings give them power and the ability to glide.
Visualize your own feathered cloak to help you connect with owl energy and
boost your personal power.

1 Picture the cloak in your mind—a collection of feathers of different sizes and
   hues, that blend together perfectly. See it shimmering with energy.

2 Now imagine donning the cloak. Feel it drape over your head and around your
   shoulders, cloaking you in a force field of power.

3 Draw in this invigorating energy as you inhale.

4 As you exhale, imagine the cloak growing in thickness, the feathers becoming
   inflated by the air which surrounds you.

5 Say: "I am a powerful presence in my world."

Wisdom: Ask an owl

The next time you are unsure of a course of action, or you have a problem, stop, take
a breath, and imagine you're face to face with a beautiful owl. Gaze into its eyes and
lose yourself in this moment. Ask for insight or a solution, then let your innate
wisdom rise to the surface.

Instinct: Hone your senses

Owls use all their senses to thrive. Follow suit and engage your senses in a creative
way to fire up your intuition.

Find a quiet spot and grab a pen and a blank sheet of paper; you're going to use
these to record your explorations of each sense in turn. Start with what you can see,
right now. Pick out one thing in your eyeline and really connect with it. How does it
make you feel? What does it make you think of? Write down your first impressions,
then move on to what you can hear, smell, feel, and taste. For every sense home in

one thing and look for the deeper meaning. What does it make you think of? How does it make you feel?

Take a moment to read through your musings. You'll notice that as you engage with your senses, you instinctively pick up more detail and can see beyond the surface. Your intuition flows and you may even notice psychic clues or messages coming through.

Journaling inspiration

- Reflect on how you used your intuition throughout the day. Were there moments where you feel you were guided by instinct? Maybe you stopped and asked for a sign to help you move forward.

- Consider how you could use your intuitive skills more often.

- Identify three things that you could do to develop your knowledge and wisdom.

Bee

**Dynamism • Communication
Passion • Motivation**

Bees are tiny winged miracles. They work together for the hive, each with a specific purpose, that benefits all. From cleaning out cells, finding and collecting nectar, to protecting the Queen, their mission is their passion. Dedication is key to the powerhouse that is the bee, and teamwork makes the dream work. They are a beauty to behold, both in flight and in the flower heads they visit; their bold and striking markings always make them stand out from the crowd.

Like the bee, you too can be fueled by your passion. Connecting with their energy can give you the drive to succeed and even to exceed your expectations. From communicating your unique message to others through harnessing your talents and skills, the power of the bee will lift you to new heights.

Your daily intention

"Today I am like a busy bee that rests upon each flower and gathers its bounty. I am alert, focused, and ready to use my skills and talents."

Set your daily intention using the morning mantra and this bee-inspired exercise.

1 Visualize yourself at the end of the day feeling pleased that you have reached all your goals.

2 See and feel the smile on your face. Know that your day has been a success.

3 Take a deep breath in and hum your joy. Draw the sound from deep in your belly as you exhale and let it vibrate through your chest and throat, like a buzzing bee.

4 To finish, state your morning mantra: "Today I am like a busy bee that rests upon each flower and gathers its bounty. I am alert, focused, and ready to use my skills and talents."

Bee folklore

Around the world the bee is a symbol of hard work, energy, and prosperity. To the ancient Mayans the bee was sacred and prized for its honey. Associated with life and energy, they even had a bee god called Ah Muzen Cab, who governed bee-keeping and was often depicted with wings.

The ancient Greeks also revered this tiny bug, believing it had divine powers. The Melissae were a group of priestesses who would gather in the temple of Demeter and perform rites in honor of the bee. Their name is a nod to the nymph Melissa, who was gifted with the secrets of bee-keeping and fed honey to the infant god Zeus.

The Celts believed that the bee was a spiritual messenger, able to travel between worlds, and the ancient tradition of "telling it to the bees" is thought to have Celtic origins. According to folklore, it was customary to tell the bees of any important event, such as births, deaths, and marriages, as a mark of respect.

Folklore fix

Take a beeswax candle and carve your initials into the wax. Say "By the power of the bee, boost my energy, bless me with success, and help me be the best!" Light the candle and watch the flame grow in length and brightness.

My enthusiasm and passion help me reach my goals.

Passion: Relive the memory

Give yourself a break during your day. Stop and bring to mind something you enjoy doing, maybe a pastime or hobby, or even something you've achieved in the past. Imagine that you are doing this thing right now. For example, if you love riding your bike, you might picture yourself riding through a beautiful park. Relive everything about this moment by engaging all your senses. Think about what you can see, hear, smell, feel, and taste. Also think about your emotions. How does it make you feel? For example, you might feel alive and full of enthusiasm, or passionate and determined. Enjoy reliving the experience and let it recharge your passion for life.

Dynamism: Concoct an elixir

Honey is the bee's gift to humankind. Not only does it taste amazing, but it's also enriched with nutrients and antibacterial properties, making it one of nature's superfoods. Connect with the power of the bee by enjoying honey when you can.

1 Pop a chamomile tea bag into a mug, cover with boiling water, and add a spoonful of honey.

2 Stir slowly, while thinking ahead to all the things you'd like to achieve.

3 Once the elixir has cooled, sip and repeat your daily affirmation in your head.

Motivation: Waggle your wings

Bees like to move, from flying long distances at top speed, to putting a wiggle in their wings with the waggle dance, which tells other bees where the best nectar is. Take a leaf out of their book and get moving. Stick on your favorite dance track and strut your stuff for a couple of minutes. Give your body a good shake and recharge your motivation.

Communication: Connect with your hive

Consider your hive, the people closest to you, those you see and work with every day. You might not get along with everyone, all of the time, but you can learn to communicate better by appreciating each other's strengths and talents.

On a piece of paper, draw a circle for each person in your hive. Add petals around the circle to create a simple flower-head diagram. Write the name of the person in the central circle. For each petal, think of a quality, talent, or skill that this person has that makes them special. It could be anything from being a good listener to being organized. Work through the flowers until you've covered everyone, then take a minute to read what you've written and appreciate each of your coworkers and friends for who they are. You'll find that when you see the big picture and value the things that set you apart, you're able to communicate more effectively and get the best out of each other.

MEDITATION

Let the bee's industry boost your mood with this gentle meditation.

Imagine it's a glorious summer's day. You're sitting on the grass, in a beautiful meadow surrounded by wildflowers. There's a gentle breeze in the air, and it's making all the fragrant blooms dance. You recline on your blanket and close your eyes, and that's when you notice the gentle humming sound. It's a soothing melody that seems to hover above your head. You recognize that it's the sound of a tiny honeybee happy in her work. You focus on the buzzing noise of her wings and feel the rhythm steady your breathing. You smile and feel the joy seeping under your skin, lifting your heart. Breathe, relax, and feel the pleasure of being at one with nature.

Journaling inspiration

- Reflect on your passions in life. What excites you? Make a list of the things that give you a buzz.

- Make another list of things you'd like to try that make you feel excited.

- Resolve to try at least one new thing and to make sure you incorporate some of your existing passions into your routine.

Rainbow

Hope • Vibrancy • Love • Empathy

Unexpectedly and seemingly from nowhere, the beautiful arc of the rainbow emerges, taking center stage in the sky. With its vibrant hues that seem to twinkle in the sunshine, it is a symbol of hope, a reminder that even when the rain comes there is always something to be thankful for.

There's a feeling of exuberance, the promise of joy to come, and also love, because nothing could be more lovely than the sight of a rainbow, however long it lasts. Connecting with such a miracle can imbue you with optimism and compassion for others. It can help you look for the positives in life and feel the love all around.

Your daily intention

"Today I will be like a beautiful rainbow; I will radiate hope and let my true colors shine brightly."

Set your intention for the day ahead and harness your inner light using this mantra.

1 Stand with feet hip-width apart, shoulders relaxed.

2 Take a breath in, and as you exhale slowly lower your body from the waist to the floor to create an arc shape.

3 Touch your toes or let your arms hang down.

4 Take another breath in, and slowly rise up, unfurling the arc you have created.

5 Say your mantra, and imagine your body sheathed in rainbow light: "Today I will be like a beautiful rainbow; I will radiate hope and let my true colors shine brightly."

Rainbow folklore

Around the world, the rainbow is synonymous with hope and healing. It is a positive symbol that comes from nowhere to lift the spirits. To the ancients it was a bridge between this world and the gods, and it had many different representations.

To the Chinese it was a two-headed dragon, a mythical beast, whose sole responsibility was to relay messages from the mortals to the heavens. The Norse named it Bifröst, the Rainbow Bridge, which linked the earth to Asgard, the realm of the gods. People of the Native American Navajo tribe see the rainbow as a serpent and a deliverer of wisdom. If you are lucky enough to see it, you should ride the beast to the spiritual realm and receive guidance and blessings.

Associated with love, good fortune, and divine wisdom, the rainbow is known for its transformative powers, which can bring positive change.

Folklore fix

Send wishes of love to lost loved ones and even those who are in need of healing here on earth, by picturing a rainbow in your mind. Imagine sending your love along the rays of light to your nearest and dearest.

Love: Rainbow shower

Need an instant pick-me-up? Wherever you are, imagine you're standing beneath a gorgeous rainbow. It emanates rays of light which are filled with loving energy. As you breathe in, you can feel this light hit the top of your head, travel down your spine, and wrap your entire body in rainbow energy. As you exhale, the loving vibes fill up your heart.

I have a spring in my step, and hope in my heart.

Hope: Sky gazing

The sky above your head is like an almighty canvas, a blank sheet from which shapes, patterns, and colors materialize. At any one time, the vista will be different. You cannot predict the picture but you can enjoy it first-hand every day. There might not always be a rainbow to take your breath away, but there are other delights to discover.

During your day, take a minute to gaze upward and really look at the sky. Notice the blend of hues, the streaks and shadows that dance beneath the sun's glare. Notice the clouds, too. Are they fluffy, angry, charcoal gray, or pure as snow? Play a game and give them shape and meaning. What do they represent? Even if the sky is full of thunder clouds, there is still beauty to be found. Focus all your attention on the heavenly realm. Drink in the space and embrace the potential that this canvas holds. Breathe and be hopeful.

Empathy: Create an arc of understanding

The rainbow arc meets the land to form a bridge between the sky and the earth. It's impossible to tell where it starts or finishes. It is a silent understanding between the eye, the mind, and the heart; we see, we believe, and we enjoy its presence. Empathy acts in a similar way. It connects us to each other. It helps us find beauty and common ground with those we might not necessarily agree with. We reach out with our thoughts and feelings, and we form an understanding.

- When you want to be empathic, picture a rainbow bridge extending from the center of your chest, to form a link between your heart and the person you're with.

- See the colors grow more vibrant and imagine sending love and understanding along each ray of light.

Vibrancy: Brighten your world

The pretty palette of rainbow colors combine to bring pleasure to the eye. Each hue is imbued with positive energy, which you can use to lift your spirits and boost your aura, the energy field that surrounds your body.

Find an image of a beautiful rainbow in nature and gaze at it. As you study the colors, ask yourself which one feels the most "positive" to you. Is there a hue that stands out, and seems to shine more brightly than the rest? Pick the color you're drawn to and imagine breathing it in for a few minutes. How do you feel? Now think about your surroundings, whether at work or at home. How can you bring more of that shade into your life? Maybe a lick of paint, a vibrant piece of art, or just a few accessories would work.

. . . .

MEDITATION

Journey the length of the rainbow, and let it soothe you from the inside out.

Imagine that before you is a stunning rainbow. You move toward it, and as you do so the ribbons of light sparkle, becoming even more vivid with every step. You can see the edge of the rainbow. It is so close; you can almost touch it. You take a deep breath and stride onto the arc. The tendrils of light respond to your touch and become solid, forming a bridge that takes you across the sky. Your feet glide. There is no effort here. It feels as though you are flying. Gently you move up and then down the other side. You find that with ease you reach the end of the rainbow, the treasure that so many have searched for. Gracefully you land, each foot cushioned by the earth. You feel calm and totally relaxed. Stand for a moment and drink in this tranquility. Let it infuse every breath you take.

. . . .

Journaling inspiration

- Think about your day and make a note of all the positive things that have happened to you.

- Even if you can think of nothing, consider what makes you feel hopeful.

- Look at the areas of your life where you could be more positive, and think of three ways that you could action this.

CHAPTER 2

The Element of Earth

Earth

There is nothing more pleasing than pressing your feet into moist grass. As the quivering blades mold to each sole, you sense that you are anchored to the earth, held in place by invisible roots. You can draw strength and solace from the knowledge that there is balance to be found when you turn your attention to the ground. All you have to do is drop your weight into each foot and bring your center of gravity down, and you will feel how much the earth supports you. Life nestles deep in the belly of the earth. Shoots take root and draw succor from their surroundings. All manner of creatures find their home here. It is a place of comfort and safety.

The Earth element is fixed and steady. It provides security and strength, a good foundation from which any living thing can grow and explore. The creatures that walk the earth, including you, can rely on its presence and beauty, from towering oaks to the tiniest acorn; a fragile flower taking its first sip of air, or a squirrel scampering along the forest floor, foraging for nuts among the fall leaves. The earth is rich with treasures, which you can experience first-hand by taking a walk in the countryside and being present in the moment.

Within this chapter you will find a selection of nature's blessings associated with the Earth element. Connecting with each of these gifts will help you find strength, balance, and flexibility, while also triggering your creative side. The suggested tips and rituals help to foster resilience and unleash your natural beauty. You'll also discover a deep sense of peace as you draw closer to the earth's bounty.

EARTH ACTIVITIES

To help you connect with this element, try to incorporate some of these activities into your schedule.

- Stand barefoot on a patch of grass
- Plant some flowers
- Take a walk in the woods
- Pick up trash in your local park
- Find a beautiful meadow and have a picnic
- Sit beneath the boughs of a tree and meditate
- Go on a nature trail
- Start your own vegetable patch

Flower Bud

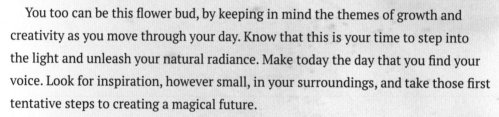

**Growth • Inspiration • Creativity
Natural beauty**

The tiny flower bud responds to the light of each new day. Slowly, steadily, it unfurls, breaking through the earth to greet the sun. It turns its face upward and accepts the warmth, letting the sun's rays permeate its being. It is open to possibility, ready to reach skyward and be the best and brightest version of itself.

You too can be this flower bud, by keeping in mind the themes of growth and creativity as you move through your day. Know that this is your time to step into the light and unleash your natural radiance. Make today the day that you find your voice. Look for inspiration, however small, in your surroundings, and take those first tentative steps to creating a magical future.

Your daily intention

"Today I shall be like a tiny flower bud, breaking through the surface of the soil to feel the warmth of the sun."

Use the mantra to set your intention for the day with the following ritual.

1 Sit on the edge of your bed and press your feet into the floor, close your eyes, and imagine you're a tiny flower bud.

2 Draw a deep breath in, and as you exhale speak the mantra aloud, with feeling: "Today I shall be like a tiny flower bud, breaking through the surface of the soil to feel the warmth of the sun.".

3 Let the ground support you, and slowly rise, lengthening your spine and extending your arms upward.

4 Tuck your tailbone in, tighten your core muscles, and tilt your chin upward.

5 Repeat the mantra, and imagine you are greeting the sun for the first time.

Flower folklore

In folklore, flowers are imbued with magical properties. Their natural beauty means they resonate love, and they've been used as a romantic symbol and a way to show affection throughout history. The geometric patterns hidden within the petals and flower heads are thought to reveal the powerful laws of the universe. Many cultures study and meditate on certain flowers in the hope of learning these secrets. Synonymous with healing and positive energy, flowers are also associated with fairies. Some fey beings even take up residence in their favorite bloom!

Not surprisingly, flowers feature in mythologies around the world and were popular among the deities for worship and celebration. Flora was the Roman goddess of flowers, plants, and the spring. This beautiful deity came into her own during the months of May and June. It was then that she helped the crops to flourish.

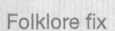

Folklore fix

Boost your positive energy and increase those happy vibes by placing a bunch of yellow blooms in a vase near your window to invite friendly spirits into your home.

Natural beauty: See beyond the surface

There's no denying that flowers are beautiful things. They come in an array of shapes, sizes, and colors. Each one is a work of art and a pleasure to the eye. Stop and take a moment to think about other things that are a pleasure to look at. It doesn't matter where you are—in the office, commuting, or at home in your kitchen—simply stop what you are doing for one minute and survey your surroundings. Focus on one thing that catches your eye. Take in its shape, size, and any unusual patterns or markings. What makes it stand out? Notice everything about this object, then commit it to memory, by closing your eyes and recreating the image in your mind.

Your senses are like muscles: the more you flex them, the stronger they become and the more you see, feel, and appreciate the world around you. By being present in the moment you will discover the hidden beauty of your surroundings.

Growth: Say "yes" to success!

Make today a "yes" day, by being open to new opportunities.

Picture your day ahead in your mind. How would you like to feel? Full of energy? Happy? Calm? See yourself acting this way as you move through your day. Watch as you complete all your tasks with ease and notice how satisfied you feel as you meet each goal. Be creative and throw in a few curveballs, so for example you might meet a new person at work, take a different route on your morning commute, or try a new class at the gym. Be excited about your day and say "yes" to whatever comes your way.

By fostering an open and positive attitude, you allow yourself to grow and radiate beauty, like a flower in nature.

Inspiration: Look up

At any point in your day, when you're feeling stressed or depleted of energy, be like the flower bud and seek out the warmth and light of the sun. If possible, go for a walk around the block or in your local park. Lift your head and let the light of the sun bathe your face. Even on the gloomiest day, looking up can help you see things from a different perspective. Take a deep breath in and draw the energizing rays of sunlight into your chest. As you breathe out, imagine this light emanating from your skin.

I grow brighter and lighter with every breath that I take.

Creativity: Doodle and dream

Doodling is a great way to engage your creative brain, and it can also help you generate and nurture ideas. The act of putting pen to paper allows your subconscious to speak through the images you create, and it's also lots of fun, so ideal for those moments when you need a break from routine.

Flowers are popular doodles. The loops of the petals and the round face are easy to draw, and you can get lost in the flow of the ink.

Take a sheet of paper and have a go at doodling a flower. Don't worry what it looks like; instead engage your subconscious. Let your fingers create a floral pattern without thinking too much about the practical side. Focus on what a flower means to you. What does it represent? When you think of your favorite flower, how does it make you feel? Connect with your emotions, as you doodle.

When you've finished, write down the first words that come into your head. These could be descriptive words associated with the flower, feelings, or even abstract ideas. Take a step back from the picture and look at what you've created. You may see the spark of an idea emerging or feel inspired, but even if you don't, you should feel energized and ready to enjoy the rest of your day.

· ·

MEDITATION

Find somewhere comfortable to sit. Close your eyes and let your body relax. Feel the weight of the day drop from your shoulders as you breathe deeply.

Imagine you're a tiny bud, poised to unfurl. You can feel the sun's rays enticing you to open up, the warmth of the spring breeze supporting and caressing you. You know that your body is nourished and supported by your surroundings. With every breath you take, you draw in the energy of the natural world. You feel it bristling under your skin, recharging you from the inside out. The worries and cares of the day slip back down, deep into the earth, where they're absorbed and transformed into positive energy. You know that whatever happens, your roots will always hold you, and keep you safe and strong. Breathe and enjoy this moment of tranquility.

· ·

Journaling inspiration

- Make a list of all the creative things you've done today, including even simple things such as creating a meal for you and your family to enjoy. Be inspired by what you have achieved.

- Come up with a list of creative ideas that you can incorporate into each day.

Stag

Tenacity • Inner strength
Magic • Steadiness

The enigmatic stag takes center stage. He moves with force and focus but is deeply connected to the earth that sustains him. He is lord of the forest and leader of the herd, and his strength comes in quiet determination. There is an awe about him. Those who are blessed enough to come face to face with such a creature never forget the experience or the magic that seeps from his presence.

You too can experience this power first-hand, by taking this blessing to heart. You can reconnect with nature and forge bonds that will hold you steady during trying times. Running with the stag brings resilience, strength, and the ability to feel your own magic within.

Your daily intention

"Today I will be like a majestic stag; I will stand my ground with strength and purpose, and I will respect the earth and all its creatures."

Set your intention for the day by repeating your mantra outside.

1 Stand barefoot outside on a patch of soil or grass. Breathe, tilt your chin up toward the sun, and connect with your surroundings.

2 Imagine you're drawing in the power of the earth through your feet.

3 Drink in the sights and sounds. Notice what you can smell, feel, and taste.

4 Say the mantra out loud or in your head, enjoying the experience of being outside at the start of the day: "Today I will be like a majestic stag; I will stand my ground with strength and purpose, and I will respect the earth and all its creatures."

Stag folklore

A symbol of transformation and magic, the stag was revered by many ancient tribes. The Celts, in particular, believed in its power and ability to provide and protect. They used every part of the beast, to make clothing, shelter, and tools, and for sustenance. The color of the stag was highly symbolic. If it was red, it belonged to the fairies, and was likely a shapeshifter or a creature of great enchantment. If it was white, it was sacred and pure of spirit. Following this stag might lead you into the fey otherworld, or some other mystical realm.

Folklore fix

Light a green candle to represent your connection to the wild places in nature. As it burns, make a wish for strength and power.

The Celtic god of wild beasts and nature, Cernunnos, was associated with the stag and often pictured with antlers. He was known as the Horned One, and it's thought he had the power to mediate between animals and humans. Herne the hunter is another version of this deity. He leads the Wild Hunt and haunts the British countryside.

Magic: Let your antlers grow!

Connect to the magic around you by reaching out with your antlers.

1 As you breathe, turn your attention to the top of your head, where your crown chakra is located. This chakra is associated with your higher self and the subconscious.

2 Each time you exhale, picture strands of light emerging from your scalp. They twist like antlers, extending into the world.

3 Imagine these antlers connecting you to other people and to the power of the universe.

4 Feel the magical energy traveling along each strand, passing messages and insights to your subconscious mind.

MEDITATION

Use this enchanting visualization to connect with the wonder of nature.

Picture yourself at the edge of a wood. You can see chinks of light between the trees. You can smell the rich, mossy undergrowth and feel the damp air against your skin. You walk slowly into the trees, all the time listening for creatures rustling in the shadows. In the distance you see a flicker of movement, and you realize that something is making its way toward you. You hold your breath as a large stag appears, standing in your path. For a second your eyes connect, and you feel a wave of energy pass between you. It's as if time is standing still, measuring this moment. The stag  *shakes his enormous antlers, bows his head, and darts in the opposite direction. You watch him run, wishing that you could follow in his path. As you drink in the wonder of this place and what just happened, a flutter of excitement settles in your chest.*

I am nurtured by nature, held safe by the earth.

Inner strength: Breathe in power

Caught in the heart of the forest, in a moment of stillness, the stag is poised. It holds itself with fearless grace, thanks to the immense power it carries within. Draw on your own inner reserves of strength, by using your breath to remain strong and present.

Take a deep breath in and imagine you're drawing it up through your body. Count out four long beats, then exhale, releasing the breath back into the ground. Continue to repeat this cycle, focusing all your attention on each breath. After a minute, extend the rhythm to five long beats. Feel the difference this makes, as you draw in more vibrant energy. Imagine the air is a conduit, allowing the inner strength you have to reach every part of your body and mind. To finish, extend the beat to six, for one final breath.

Tenacity: Switch up your skills

The stag demonstrates tenacity during the rutting season when it goes up against other males. Not one to shy away from competition, it uses all the tools it has to win favor with the hinds. Adopt a tenacious spirit like the stag by switching up your skill set.

Make two lists, the first highlighting the skills you already have, the second noting the skills you'd like to learn. Go through the first list and think of something you could do to enhance each skill. For example, if you're good with words, you could take a creative writing course.

Next consider the list of skills you'd like. How important is each one? Number them in order, then, starting with the most important, think of something you could do to develop that skill.

Pin the lists you've created somewhere you'll see them every day. When you master something on the list, tick it off.

Steadiness: Stamp your hooves

Turn your attention to the soles of your feet. Press them deep into the ground and feel the connection. Drop your weight into your knees and imagine you're making an indentation with each sole. Dig in from the heel and let each foot roll forward so that the weight travels through to the ball and your toes. Know that you are held steady, each foot securely in place. Breathe and let the vibration of the earth's natural rhythms ground you.

Journaling inspiration

- How have you connected with nature today? Perhaps you took a walk in the park, or did some gardening. Maybe you spent some time listening to the birds, or just noticed the changes in the weather. List the ways that you engaged with the natural world, and how this made you feel.
- Identify new ways of connecting with nature that fit in with your daily routine.

Mountain

Ambition • Resilience • Presence • Self-belief

Breathtaking, beautiful, and sometimes treacherous, mountains are an impressive part of the natural world. Born from changes as the earth evolved, they steadily emerged over time to find their place in the landscape, and also our hearts. They are symbols of resilience and strength, particularly for those who wish to conquer them. Once at the top, you're sure to get a spectacular view, allowing you to experience the earth from a different perspective.

You too can be a magnificent mountain, stepping into your personal power and making your mark, by manifesting strength and resilience. Take the themes of this blessing to heart in your approach to everyday tasks. Stand tall and be proud of your accomplishments.

Your daily intention

"Today I shall be like a mountain, rising up from the valley to command the view with my presence and power."

Set your intention for the day, using the morning mantra and this simple stretching exercise.

1 Crouch down on the floor in a ball, take a deep breath in, and slowly unfurl until you are in a standing position.

2 As you exhale, lengthen and stretch your spine and raise your arms above your head.

3 Tuck your bottom in and imagine a thread tugging your head upward.

4 Stand tall and proud.

5 Repeat your mantra loudly, as if you were shouting it from the mountain top:

"Today I shall be like a mountain, rising up from the valley to command the view with my presence and power."

Mountain folklore

Mountains feature in myths and legends around the world. They rise up from the ground, a magnificent force of nature. They are unstoppable, immovable, a solid presence which can be seen as an obstacle, or a challenge. There is something remote and sacred about them too, for they span both the earthly realm and the heavens above. As such, they are channels of magic, and a link to holy beings. Many pilgrims have journeyed to the mountain peak in search of the divine wisdom of the gods.

According to Greek legend, Mount Olympus was home to the Olympians, a super-race of deities who liked to meddle in the affairs of humans. They would sit on their thrones and watch as life played out on earth. To speak to the gods, one might have to perform the impossible and climb the mountain, or at least petition them for blessings.

Folklore fix

Take a large brown pillar candle to symbolize the mountain and carve your initials into the wax. Light the candle and make a wish for success.

Many ancient cultures believed the mountain to be the center of the world, a dwelling place of the gods, and a sacred portal. In Nepal, Everest is known as "the Mother Goddess of the World" and also the "Navel of the Water."

Self-belief: Piece it together

Everything is connected, like a jigsaw puzzle. Just as the mountain is connected to the valley below, and part of a much bigger landscape, so are the cities and towns and the bricks and concrete a part of the urban environment. One thing blends into another, but each piece makes up the picture we see.

Take a moment during your day to see how the pieces fit in your world. Each part of your life, from home and family, to your social life, friends, career, and dreams, is a piece that makes up the jigsaw of you. Ask yourself how it all fits together. Are some pieces bigger than others? Are some less important? Perhaps you've not been paying enough attention to a piece and you need to redress the balance. Spending a few mindful minutes reflecting on the bigger picture and how it all fits together can help you find the focus and drive to move forward.

Resilience: One foot in front of the other

Adopt a tenacious spirit by taking a step-by-step approach.

Start your day with this visualization. Picture yourself at the base of a mountain. You can see a path etched into the landscape. It curves around the peak, leading to the summit. You stride forward with confidence and begin to climb the mountain. For every step you take, your power increases and you pick up speed. Each footfall leaves an indentation as you press on, and your steps become so fast that you're almost running. Eventually, you reach the top, throw your arms open wide, and say, "One foot in front of the other, I make my way!"

I stand tall and rise up to meet new challenges.

Presence: Embrace space, height, and distance

To boost personal power at any point during the day, take time out and put some distance between yourself and the rest of the world. Imagine you're standing at the top of a mountain. You're miles away from everything, standing on the pinnacle. Embrace the space, take a long, deep breath of mountain air, and feel the strength of your vitality.

Ambition: Climb the mountain

Use a creative exercise to help you find the strength you need to reach your goals and targets. You'll need a large piece of paper and some pens. Draw a mountain on the page, with a wide foundation at the bottom and a point at the top to represent the pinnacle. At the peak of the mountain, write one word to represent your goal. Now draw lines like steps all the way up the mountain. For each step, think of one thing that might help you reach your goal. For example, if your goal is to get a promotion at work, you might compile a portfolio of all the experience you have, single out any standout projects that have been successful, and highlight any qualifications that might help. Think also of new steps you can take, such as taking a new course, or shadowing someone who is already in the job you want.

Look at the image you've created and imagine climbing that mountain for real. Focus on what you want to achieve. See yourself reaching the top and imagine how that will feel.

MEDITATION

Let go of stress and relax by traveling to the heart of the mountain with this simple visualization.

Close your eyes. Imagine you're standing before a cave carved into the mountainside. You can see a light flickering inside. It looks warm and sheltered from the outside world, so you move toward the glow. The warmth envelops you and you feel safe. The stone walls rise up around you and you reach out, feeling the smoothness of the grain against your skin. You sense the timeless power of the mountain; it permeates your being. You take a deep breath in and draw down the energy of this place. You can feel it settle in your belly, soothing any fear. You stand at the heart of the mountain, calm, rooted, and relaxed.

Journaling inspiration

- List the highs and lows of your day.

- When did you feel as though you were at the foot of the mountain, and when did you feel as though you'd conquered it? What helped you reach the top?

- Highlight three things that give you strength and resilience.

Rabbit

**Ingenuity • Openness
Adaptability • Grounding**

Rabbits have a strong connection with the earth.
They make their homes there, burrowing deep beneath
the surface to find warmth, shelter, and security. Often
considered fearful creatures, rabbits live by their wits and intuition. They
instinctively read the atmosphere and react swiftly, whether that's to partake in
spontaneous fun or flee at top speed.

These social animals can teach us much about the way we interact with each other
and the world around us. Connecting with rabbit energy will help you stay grounded,
but open to possibility. You'll learn how to hone your intuition, and trust that you
have all the answers. You'll also begin to see wonder in the mundane, and discover
that adventure is simply a hop, skip, and jump away!

Your daily intention

*"Today I will be like a rabbit; I will trust my instincts and embrace my
playful side, while staying connected to the earth."*

Use your morning mantra with a simple exercise to generate energy and enthusiasm
for the day ahead.

1 Stand on the spot and press your heels into the floor. Drop your weight into your
knees and bounce lightly on the spot.

2 Repeat the morning mantra as you bob up and down: "Today I will be like a rabbit;
I will trust my instincts and embrace my playful side, while staying connected to
the earth."

3 Now increase the speed and begin to make small jumps or hops.

4 Throw your arms up in the air or let them hang loose. Have a bit of fun and
freestyle it.

5 Continue jumping for a minute, then slow things down and return to a standing position.

6 Repeat the mantra once more, with feeling!

Rabbit folklore

Rabbits feature in mythologies around the world and are often associated with the moon. The Celts considered them sacred, and would study the patterns of their tracks on the ground and follow their mating rituals. They held hares and bunnies in such high regard that they seldom ate their meat.

In ancient Greece the rabbit was a symbol of love, fertility, and abundance. Associated with the goddess Aphrodite, bunnies were often given as romantic tokens, while in Rome they were presented to a married woman to help her conceive.

In some native traditions the rabbit was the trickster character, from Cherokee tales of mischief-making rabbits to Brer Rabbit of the American South, a smart, quick-thinking opponent who used his intuition to outsmart his enemies. As a totem, the rabbit teaches us to face our fears, use our

Folklore fix

To attract good fortune, place an image of a rabbit by your front door. Every time you pass through the door, make a wish for abundance.

senses to read situations, and react with flexibility. A global symbol of good luck, rabbits can help strengthen our connection with the earth and attract abundance.

Ingenuity: Trigger the trickster

Trigger your inner trickster and learn to think on your feet, by setting yourself a multi-tasking challenge.

Take a grocery list and try to memorize each item, but in true rabbit style, get moving: jog on the spot while running through the items, for example, "carrot, lettuce, apples." Set a timer for three minutes and continue to jog and recite the list. When your time is up, rest for a minute, then see how many of the items you can remember. Repetition is key with this exercise, so keep practicing and you should notice that you'll be able to retain more information and recall it quickly.

Grounding: Spread your roots deep

Rabbits like to dig. They enjoy the connection they have with the earth. They feel safe and secure when cocooned deep in their burrows. Be more bunny and get to grips with the dirt beneath your feet.

Find a patch of moist soil—maybe in your garden, or in a planter—and dig your fingers in. Scoop up the earth gently. Feel it gather in the palm of each hand. Mold it, and massage it between your fingers. Dig your hands in further and let them explore. Imagine your fingers are the spreading roots of a plant or tree. Embrace the connection and know that you are anchored by the earth. Draw in a deep breath and feel the energy travel through your hands and wrists, up your arms, and into your body.

Openness: Turn the critic into the cheerleader

Be open to opportunity and ready for anything by using positive keywords to reprogram your inner critic. When you notice your inner voice being negative about something you're about to do, take a breath and say, "stop." Then repeat, "I can, I am, and I will."

I live in the moment and engage
with my surroundings.

Adaptability: Reverse the view

Switch things up and practice adapting to your environment.

Go outside and lie on the ground. Press your spine into the earth and really feel your connection to the landscape. Now turn your attention to what you can see above. Look at the sky and enjoy the view. Imagine that you've been flipped upside down, so that the earth is the sky and vice versa. You are now looking down at a vast sea of sky. How does it feel to turn things on their head and have a different perspective? What do you notice? You might feel uncomfortable about looking at things this way, or you might feel excited. Make a note of anything that stands out and any other observations that you have.

Being flexible means being able to shift your perspective and see things differently. When you practice doing this physically, you also exercise your mental ability to be adaptable and move beyond what is normal for you.

MEDITATION

Feel the joy with this simple bunny-inspired visualization.

You're standing in a beautiful walled garden, with an abundance of flowers. The sweet scents of rose and honeysuckle fill the air. The lawn is lush and green, moist from the early-morning dew. A movement catches your eye: something small and fluffy, darting to the left. You follow with your gaze and that's when you see them. Not one, not two, but a host of tiny wild rabbits' tails bobbing in the distance. You follow them, watching as they skip away. You smile and feel the playful joy that passes between them. It lifts your spirits, and for a moment you wish you were with them, frolicking in the grass. Instead you delight at their antics and appreciate the beauty of the natural world. Breathe and enjoy these happy vibes.

Journaling inspiration

- Reflect on your day and some of the challenges you faced. Were you fearful or open and adaptable?

- Think of three ways that you can be more open and flexible in your daily or weekly routine.

Tree

Generosity • Persistence • Flexibility • Ancestral wisdom

Timeless sentinels, trees are the guardians of the forest, anchored deep within the earth. Connected by a network of roots and branches, they work together and for each other. They communicate, sending nourishment and healing to the sick and fallen among them. They give to all the creatures of the earth, withstanding the elements and the pressure of time.

One of nature's most precious teachers, trees can help us reach out, forge links with each other, and be generous in heart and mind. They can show us how to weather the storm, standing resolute and yet leaning into the breeze. There is wisdom to be found in the pattern of the bark and there are secrets to discover in the rustle of leaves, if you're prepared to dig deep.

Your daily intention

"Today I will be like a mighty tree. I will spread my roots, branch out in search of new connections, and draw strength from the earth that supports me."

Combine your morning mantra with an energizing exercise to start the day right.

1 Bend down low, so that you're bouncing on your feet with your knees bent.

2 Go into a deep lunge and hold the position to the count of three.

3 Take a deep breath in, and as you exhale return to a standing position.

4 Repeat the lunge three times, extending the beat by one each time, as you hold the position.

5 As you come out of your final lunge, reach upward and imagine that your arms and hands are branches reaching for the stars.

6 Shout your mantra aloud: "Today I will be like a mighty tree. I will spread my roots, branch out in search of new connections, and draw strength from the earth that supports me."

Tree folklore

The Celts believed that every living thing had a spirit, an energy which could be tapped into. To them, trees were sacred and associated with wisdom and strength. The sound of the breeze whispering in the leaves was considered the music of the gods, and trees provided a conduit between this world and the spiritual plane.

To the ancients around the world, trees were magical, having the power to live for thousands of years and regenerate while nurturing the planet at the same time. The ancient Greeks believed in Dryads, beautiful nymphs who made their home in a specific tree and were charged with its protection. These enigmatic tree spirits could only venture so far from the tree of their dwelling. The Sumerians, meanwhile, prized the cedars of Lebanon, believing them to be the home of the gods.

Ancestral wisdom: Step back in time

Having been around for hundreds of years, trees have learned much from each other and their environment. Take a leaf out of their book and reach into the past to build for the future.

Folklore fix

Find a large tree and sit beneath its boughs. Lean against the trunk and breathe in its energy. Look up and whisper your most precious wish into the canopy.

Spend some mindful time thinking about those who have gone before. Look to your immediate family, and loved ones who have passed, and consider the lessons they have taught you. Bring to mind qualities that you admire in these people and consider how you can adopt these. Spend time looking at old photographs, to help you reconnect with memories and older relatives. Write a list of questions you can ask your living relations to get a better understanding of your ancestors. As you delve deeper into the past, you'll recognize family traits and lessons you've learned, and the thread of ancestral wisdom will emerge.

Generosity: Get your hands dirty

Cultivate a generous spirit by planting and nurturing seeds. You can exercise your green fingers whether you've a yard or allotment, or even just a windowsill where you can place a plant pot. All you need is a pot, compost, and some seeds or a bulb of your choice.

1 Dig deep into the earth with your hands and scoop out a space for your plant to grow.

2 Enjoy the sensation of the soil between your fingers and notice how it makes you feel.

3 Plant the seed or bulb into the hollow you've created, then cover it with more compost.

4 To finish, sprinkle with water.

5 Each time you water your plant, observe any changes and enjoy watching it grow.

Flexibility: Bend and twist

Trees weave with the wind, rather than resisting the flow. Their roots allow them a degree of movement while holding them in place. When you need to be flexible in mind, be flexible in body. Secure your feet upon the ground. Imagine you have roots that anchor you in place, then twist from the waist in both directions. Each time you twist, pick up speed and stretch even further, but keep your feet firmly in place.

Each day, I expand my wisdom, strength, and flexibility.

Persistence: Build a tree

Consider the things you'd like to achieve. You might have a number of different goals, personal and career-related. To develop the persistence you need to work toward each one—imagine you're building a tree.

Take a large sheet of paper and start with a sturdy trunk to represent you right now. Each goal then becomes a branch which stems from this trunk. Write your goal along the main body of the branch using a few keywords. Each branch can have a number of twigs, and these are the steps you can take to help you reach your goal. Again, use keywords and write these steps along the twigs.

Finally, consider your roots, the core values, talents, and qualities that give you the resilience you need to reach your goals. Add the roots to your picture and note down what they represent.

This is your tree of resilience. Looking at it will help you remain strong, determined, and focused.

· ·

MEDITATION

Use this calming visualization to feel safe and sheltered from the world.

Picture a giant oak, with a thick, sturdy trunk and a mass of branches that meet above your head. Imagine sitting with your back against the bark. You can feel the vibration of the tree, the power seeping from the gnarled wood into your skin. Breathe in and draw more of that energy into your body. Breathe out and pour all of your fear and negativity into the earth, where it can be born anew. As you relax, you feel your body sink deeper into the trunk. It feels as though you are falling into the tree, as much a part of it as the roots and branches. The oak supports you; it provides shelter, protection, and a safe place where you can be yourself. Relax and enjoy this sense of belonging.

· ·

Journaling inspiration

- Trees are anchored by their roots, but what anchors you? Perhaps you have a safe place, somewhere that you go to recharge or find peace? Maybe it's a certain person, or something that you do, that helps. Identify your anchors and list them.

- If you can, think of some new anchors and add them to the list.

Stone

Strength • Insight
Authenticity • Transformation

Most stone was born when the mineral gases that made up
the earth cooled and solidified. As such, its core is dense and
unyielding, a robust force that can withstand elemental
and environmental changes. Despite its sturdy presence,
stone wears the scars of transformation with veins and
indentations. Whether it is large and rocky or smooth and
pebble-like, it has a story to tell.

Like stone, we can also remain stoic and strong in the
face of adversity. We can weather the changes and come out
the other side, with wisdom that adds to our natural beauty.
Channeling the energy of stone will help you step into your power and develop inner
reserves of strength to carry you through any transformation.

Your daily intention

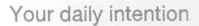

*"Today I will be a stone, solid and smooth but etched by the grains of the
earth. I will remain true to my vision, a rock with strong foundations."*

Find your inner core of strength and set your daily intention using the mantra
with a simple exercise.

1 Sit on the edge of your bed and place both hands palm down just below your belly
button. This area is home to the sacral chakra, the seat of your personal power.

2 Imagine a stone nestled here. As you breathe, feel the stone increase in size and
strength. Notice its solidity and how it helps you feel connected to the earth.

3 Say your mantra aloud and enjoy feeling grounded: "Today I will be a stone, solid
and smooth but etched by the grains of the earth. I will remain true to my vision,
a rock with strong foundations."

Stone folklore

To the ancients around the world, stone is sacred. It is the bones of the landscape, the soul of the earth from which all things spring forth. Crafted into monuments and tablets, used to mark burial sites and places of ritual magic, stone is at the heart of some of the oldest traditions.

The Celts believed that everything had a spiritual energy, a force which could be worked with, and stone was no exception. Protruding from the earth's surface, those ancient stone monuments connected all three realms, from the earth to the underworld and the heavenly realm of the sky.

Stone was often used as a clan symbol by the Native Americans and featured in many of their myths and legends, from Blackfoot tales about a magic Buffalo Stone, to the Mi'kmaq legend of the ancient rock that became the first Grandmother. Stone was associated with strength and protection. Tribes with Stone Clans include the Hopi and the Pueblo Indians.

Folklore fix

Choose a beautiful stone for a paperweight. Hold it in both hands and make a wish. Write the same wish on some paper and place it beneath the stone until it is granted!

Strength: Be still as stone

Tap into your inner strength by combining a breathing exercise with good posture.

1 Stand or sit with your feet hip-width apart.

2 Breathe in and lengthen your spine.

3 Feel your feet pressing firmly into the floor.

4 As you exhale, count to five and let your shoulders drop.

5 Take another long, deep breath and tilt your chin upward. Tighten your stomach and feel your core harden.

6 Imagine that in this moment you're made of stone. Feel the strength and stability this brings.

7 Breathe and enjoy the stillness.

. . . .

MEDITATION

Feel centered and calm with this powerful "stone circle" meditation.

Picture yourself sitting in the middle of a stone circle. The landscape is rugged, and the air is thick with swirling mist. Giant lumps of rock sprout from the earth and smaller stones surround you in a perfect ring. You feel grounded, centered, and protected from the elements. This is a sacred place, a space where you can connect to the Earth element and draw its strength into your body and mind. You can recharge here and let go of any stress that you have gathered during your day. Focus on being at the heart of the stone circle, and every time your mind wanders, bring your attention back to the earth, to the towering stones and the sense of peace that fills the air.

. . . .

Transformation: Wishing stones

You'll need a selection of stones of roughly the same size and shape, and some permanent marker pens. Start by thinking about the qualities that are important to you, things that you'd like to have more of or to attract, for example, confidence, compassion, and joy. Make a list of these qualities, without thinking too much about it. Just let the ideas flow onto paper.

When you've finished, circle the ones that you feel are the most important, then take a marker pen and write each one on a different stone. You might also want to decorate the stones. Allow your creative side to come through and enjoy the process.

Place the finished stones in a dish face down. Every day, pick a stone and see which quality you have drawn, then consider how you can introduce more of that into your life. Think of little things you can do to change the way you think and feel, using the stone as a prompt.

Authenticity: Stone power

Go for a walk and keep your eyes peeled for interesting stones. If you see one you like, pick it up and spend five minutes sitting with it in your hands. Notice how it feels against your skin, the size, the shape, and any unusual markings. What drew you to this stone in the first place? Perhaps it reminds you of something, such as a jewel or crystal, or it stood out from the rest of the landscape. Ponder the power of the stone. It is a raw piece of nature. What you see is what you get—there are no hidden motives. A stone is a stone.

Take this time to consider your own authenticity and if you need to be more honest with yourself and others. Keep the stone as a reminder that you too are a part of nature and that you should always be true to yourself.

My core is strong, and I am true to myself.

Insight: Travel to the core

Harness inner wisdom with this quick trick. Imagine with every breath that you're tunneling to the center of the earth, scaling deeper into stone and rock to reach the core. Here you will find all the answers you seek. Close your eyes, immerse yourself in the darkness, and let the insights come.

Journaling inspiration

- Reflect on your day. Did you feel truly strong and in control at any point? Why was this?

- Consider the times you felt vulnerable and ask yourself what contributed to this feeling.

- Consider the little things you could do to build inner strength, and the changes you could make in your daily life: for example, setting boundaries in your relationships and saying "no" sometimes.

CHAPTER 3

The Element of Fire

Fire

Fire comes with a hunger, an urgency to fill its belly. It spreads fast, the slick flames engulfing everything in its path. A catalyst for change, it burns through the mire, leaving the bare bones exposed. It is action, passion, power in its rawest form. There is danger if you get too close, but there is also something cleansing about this element. It cuts through the debris and allows a fresh start.

As a tool for transformation, there is nothing fiercer than fire. If you want to shake things up, fire ignites the spark, but there is also a gentler, nurturing side to the inferno. The warmth it provides allows comfort, the opportunity to heal and grow strong. The flames which light the hearth also cook the food. Once more the theme of change emerges. The magic that occurs during the heating process is alchemical. It is this energy that the element brings to your life.

Fire motivates. It builds slowly, from those first few sparks to the solid wall of flame that consumes everything. It is bold and vibrant, and it can teach you to be the same. Let's not forget that it is also incredibly beautiful. If you've ever gazed into flames, you will have seen an array of colors and patterns, a carnival that danced before your eyes. Fire doesn't do things by half measures. It goes full pelt to captivate your heart.

The blessings and rituals in this section will help you connect with this element. If you're feeling vulnerable, this is the place to start: reconnect with your primal spark, harness strength and courage, find your passion, and follow your heart, becoming a trailblazer for what you believe in. The power of the flame can help you re-invent yourself so that you will always burn bright.

FIRE ACTIVITIES

To help you connect with this element, try to incorporate some of these activities into your schedule.

- Light a candle and gaze at the flame

- Go outside and watch the sunrise

- Sit and relax by an open fire

- Go outside and watch the sunset

- Soak up the sun by sunbathing, or simply close your eyes and turn your face to the sunshine

- Gather with friends and family around a bonfire

- Take in the magnificent wonder of a lightning storm

- Perform a sun salute (see page 80) as the sun rises

Sun

Vitality • Confidence
Kindness • Self-love

There is no denying the sun's life-giving power. This fiery orb is at the center of all things, having an impact on everything from seasonal changes to the crops we grow, the length of each day, and how we feel as we journey upon this earth. The glorious light and warmth it provides are always present. It never stops shining, even on the dullest of days.

You too can be like the sun. You have a light within which you can share with others. You have a warmth, an energy that motivates and invigorates. Like the sun, you have the ability to take center stage and let the rest of the world see what you can do. The sun can help you embrace your unique talents and boost vitality, so that you can be your sparkly best at all times.

Your daily intention

"Today, I will be like the sun; I will have confidence in my own abilities and radiate light and love wherever I go."

Set your daily intention using the morning mantra and a simple sun salute.

1 Stand with feet hip-width apart, shoulders relaxed.

2 Lunge forward with your right leg and sweep your arms up straight, palms together.

3 Take a deep breath in and sweep your arms around in a circular motion until they hang at your sides. Imagine you're drawing the sun toward you.

4 Bring your other leg forward so that both legs meet, and return to a standing position.

5 Exhale, then say your mantra: "Today, I will be like the sun; I will have confidence in my own abilities and radiate light and love wherever I go."

Sun folklore

To the ancients the sun was a celestial powerhouse, casting light on the land and providing warmth. A mystical orb, its path through the sky was a source of fascination and the subject of many folk tales. When the sun disappeared, it was feared that some otherworldly creature had stolen it, but luckily it was always reborn the next day.

Sun deities feature in mythologies around the world, from the great Egyptian sun god, Ra, who sailed through the sky on his chariot, chased by the serpent demon Apep, to Sunna, the beautiful Norse goddess of the sun, pursued by the savage wolf Skoll—sometimes he got so close he'd take a bite from the sun, causing an eclipse. A universal symbol of vitality, energy, and joy, the sun is worshipped for its life-giving power, and its energy is channeled in rituals for health, healing, and confidence.

Self-love: Enjoy your reflection

Give yourself the love and attention you deserve. Take a minute out of your day and simply gaze at your reflection in the mirror. Smile and notice everything about your features, the way this one expression lifts your face and makes your eyes sparkle. Look at the shape of your face and the way your hair frames it. Stare into your eyes and fall in love with yourself. There is no one else on the planet like you. You are special, individual, unique. Consider all the things that make you stand out, and celebrate your inner beauty. Say the affirmation below, while taking in the wonder of your reflection.

Folklore fix

Leave a piece of quartz crystal in indirect sunlight for about 30 minutes to charge. Quartz retains and amplifies energy. Hold the crystal in both hands and breathe in the vitality.

I love and accept myself as I am.

Kindness: Share small kindnesses

You can give in many ways, from giving your time to offering a compliment. Consider how you can do this today with friends, coworkers, and family members. What would really make them smile and lift their spirits?

• Make a list of all the things you can do throughout your day to make others happy. Think of small kindnesses, such as holding a door open or helping someone with their groceries. Even a smile or an encouraging word can make all the difference and brighten someone's day.

• Be generous with your time. If someone needs a shoulder to cry on, or just someone to listen, be that person.

• Be there and be present.

• Be generous with yourself, too. If you need time out, take it, whether you need self-care, pampering, or just a confidence boost. Be kind to yourself.

Vitality: Turn up your shine

Imagine there's a sun-shaped thermostat in the center of your chest. Every time you turn it, your aura, the energy field around your body, gets bigger and brighter. Turn it up to feel energized and unleash your shine!

Confidence: Dance in the spotlight

Doing something creative can boost self-belief, especially if you couple this with soaking up the sun's confidence-boosting rays. Take five minutes out of your busy day to observe the patterns made by the sun.

On a sunny day, go outdoors, taking a notebook and pencil with you, and sit in the shade of a tree. Steady your breathing, focusing on the gentle rise and fall of your chest for a minute, until you feel relaxed. Use your notebook and pencil to sketch any interesting patterns you see on the ground. Alternatively, you might prefer to gaze up into the canopy and look at the sun filtering through the leaves, then recreate this image.

As you're sketching, try to make use of the sun's vibrant energy. Feel it seeping into your skin and imagine it bathing you in pretty patterns. Picture your aura—the energy field around your body—shimmering, as the dapples of light cover you from head to toe. Breathe in the warmth and confidence.

When you're done, position your drawing somewhere that you can see it and be reminded of the sun's radiance.

. . . .

MEDITATION

Recharge your energy levels with this soothing meditation.

Imagine you're sitting on a mountain watching the sun rise. You can see a glimmer of light on the horizon, then gradually the colors emerge, going from pink to orange and then vibrant yellow. The sky seems suddenly alive as the sun takes center stage. The landscape too is changing. The gentle kiss of the sun's rays makes everything look brighter. You can feel the warmth on your skin as you are bathed in sunlight. You can sense the heat filling your heart and fueling every breath that you take. Enjoy the comforting feeling of the sun's caress, as it recharges your body and mind.

Journaling inspiration

- Spend a few minutes thinking about your day. Can you pinpoint any moments when you felt confident and empowered?

- Think about these moments and consider why you felt that way. Were you doing something you loved? Perhaps you felt in control, or was it maybe because you were so involved in what you were doing?

- Make a list of things that you could do to feel more confident every day.

Lizard

Positivity • Magnetism
Psychic ability • Patience

Sleek and sinewy, the lizard has great magnetism.
With heightened senses, it is susceptible to the
slightest change in temperature, but can quickly absorb
the sun's rays and the heat from underfoot. Some even change color
so that they can take in more warmth. The charming lizard is a creature of mystery.
With patience and perseverance, it waits motionless for its prey, often almost
invisible until the time is right to strike.

Working with the blessings of the lizard can help you develop the patience you
need to reach your goals and connect with others. You'll improve your psychic
senses, so that you can identify what is right for you and learn how to maintain
and radiate positive energy.

Your daily intention

*"Today I shall be like a lizard; I will use all my senses and reach out to
others, with warmth, patience, and love."*

Use the morning mantra with a simple exercise to create positive energy for
the day ahead.

1 Stand barefoot on the floor.

2 Breathe and draw in the heat from your surroundings.

3 Even if the floor feels cold, imagine flames beneath the surface and feel the
warmth gradually taking hold.

4 Every time you inhale, draw in more of this positive energy, and feel it seeping
into your bones.

5 To finish, take a deep breath and state your mantra: "Today I shall be like a lizard; I will use all my senses and reach out to others, with warmth, patience, and love."

Lizard folklore

A symbol of sensitivity, mystery, and the psychic realms, the lizard features in mythologies around the world. This tiny creature has been a source of fascination for thousands of years. To the Native American tribes, the lizard was a positive omen, a sign of abundance to come, and also indicative of the mysteries of dreamtime—lizards were often called upon to assist in psychic journeys.

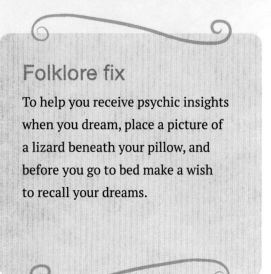

Folklore fix
To help you receive psychic insights when you dream, place a picture of a lizard beneath your pillow, and before you go to bed make a wish to recall your dreams.

The Mayans believed that the lizard had a role to play in the creation of the earth, while in Japan lizards were associated with love and fertility. In this guise, their body parts were often used in love potions, and amulets were formed in lizard-like shapes to attract a soulmate. The Japanese believed their lithe shape and movement were erotic, while to the Chinese lizards were associated with dragons and considered auspicious.

Patience: Step back and relax

Use this mindful technique to develop more patience.

If you're in a situation where you need to be more patient with someone, take a step back. You might want to do this physically, to create some space between you. As you inhale, let your focus take a step back, too. Draw your attention to the back of your head, and imagine falling into this space, then take your time and exhale. When we look at someone, we are front facing, gazing at them directly with our eyes, but by taking a step back and letting your attention relax, you'll adopt an attitude of patience. This technique also works when you need to be more patient about your goals. Take a couple of minutes out to breathe, relax your focus, and fall back into your mind.

Positivity: Make a lizard charm

Carnelian is one of the stones associated with the lizard. It is bright, vibrant, and packed with positive energy. Use the stone to help you connect with this blessing throughout your day.

1 Leave a small piece of carnelian in direct sunlight for at least 30 minutes, to absorb the warmth.

2 Collect the stone and hold it in your cupped hands.

3 Breathe in and draw the heat from the stone into your hands, along your arms, and into your body.

4 Exhale and imagine any negative energy flowing back through your palms into the stone.

5 Continue this cycle of breathing for five minutes, then return the stone to the sunlight for cleansing.

Magnetism: Radiate loving vibes

Boost your allure and share the love with this mini visualization. Like the lizard, you have the ability to radiate warmth in the form of loving vibes, which will also draw people to you. Imagine a whirling ball of pink energy in the center of your chest. See it expand until it becomes a ray of heat, which covers everything and everyone in pink light. Feel the warmth spread from your heart and visualize the color pink everywhere!

*I turn up my charm
and radiate warmth
to all I meet.*

MEDITATION

Use this heart-warming meditation to feel relaxed and upbeat.

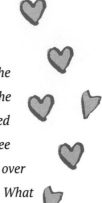

Imagine you're a lizard lapping up the sun's heat, as you lie outstretched on the sand. You can feel a blanket of warmth wrap around your body. You can feel the heat beneath you, caressing your motionless form. You are completely cocooned and relaxed. Your breath softens and you close your eyes. What color do you see when you think of the warmth that surrounds you? Imagine that shade taking over your body. Feel the color blend into your skin, as you meld with the sun's rays. What other colors do you see? Imagine your skin tone changing to reflect how you are feeling. Enjoy the sensation of being able to transform the way you look and feel.

Psychic ability: Activate your sixth sense

Lizards can detect the slightest change in temperature. Their super-honed senses pick up on this and other movements to help them survive and thrive in their environment. Follow suit and use all your senses to pick up on subtle hints and signs from the universe.

Bring your attention to your third eye chakra, which is situated in the middle of your forehead. With your index finger, lightly trace a circle in this area for a minute, to stimulate your psychic senses.

When you're relaxed and feel ready, close your eyes and picture a cinema screen in your head. Ask for a sign, or an image from the universe, then let any pictures form gradually. You might see colors, words, or patterns. Don't worry too much about what you do or don't see.

When you're ready, open your eyes and recreate what you saw on a piece of paper. You might want to draw it, describe it using words, or simply reflect on how it made you feel. Even if you didn't get a clear image, you might be left with random thoughts or a feeling. Find a way to express this on the paper.

Practice this technique often to strengthen your psychic senses.

Journaling inspiration

- How patient are you? Were there moments in your day when you could have been more patient? Isolate those times and run through each one in your mind.

- Consider how you could have been more patient. Could you have shown more compassion or taken a step back?

- Identify and write down three strategies to help you develop more patience when dealing with others.

Lightning

Focus • Illumination • Action • Self-assurance

Lightning comes swiftly and with dynamic force. It splits the sky in two, with fierce, unwavering precision. It's a spectacle of nature and often unexpected. It is breathtakingly beautiful, too. Lightning is the messenger of the gods and as such feels like a divine revelation when it strikes. It represents quick, decisive action and is a symbol of power and celestial force.

Working with this blessing will bring you bountiful rewards, from helping you see the light and take assertive action, to providing inspiration, confidence, and vitality that oozes from every pore. Lightning will get you moving in whatever direction you'd like to go.

Your daily intention

"Today I will be like the lightning; I will step into my power and act with clarity. I will make my mark."

Combine the morning mantra with this powerful visualization to make your day a success.

1 Think about your day and bring to mind the things you want to achieve. These could be small goals, such as trying a new yoga move, to bigger things like giving a work presentation.

2 See your goal as a picture framed in golden light.

3 Imagine you've a bow and arrow in your hands that fires lightning bolts. Take aim and fire at the picture. Watch as you hit your goal and the image explodes into hundreds of lightning bolts.

4 To finish, state your morning mantra: "Today I will be like the lightning; I will step into my power and act with clarity. I will make my mark."

Lightning folklore

A symbol of strength and power, lightning is a force of nature that cannot be denied. Stunning to see but lethal in its destruction, this phenomenon mesmerized the ancients, believing it to be the work of the deities. Most considered lightning to be punishment from the heavenly realms.

The ancient Greeks attributed lightning to the king of the gods, Zeus. He governed the sky and thunder, and his bolt was a mark of his immense power. In Norse mythology it was Thor who held the magic of the lightning bolt in his hands. Delivered by the strike of his mighty hammer Mjolnir, the lightning bolt was used by Thor to defend Asgard from the Giants and to keep evil at bay.

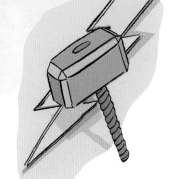

Action: Infuse your movements

Take inspiration from a flash of lightning and do some impromptu physical moves to generate energy and action.

Start by picking a body part, for example your right arm. Breathe energy into your arm by focusing your inward breath upon this area. As you exhale, move your arm in some way. Don't think too much about it, just do it! Now move on to your other arm, a leg, or a foot. Go through each body part, breathing energy into it. Have fun with this and enjoy flexing all your muscles. To finish, go crazy and throw a few shapes by moving everything at once. Imagine you're a bolt of lightning lighting up the sky with lots of erratic patterns.

When we move with freedom physically, we build momentum and sharpen our focus. This in turn affects how we feel and our thought processes, making us more likely to take action in other ways.

Folklore fix

The next time you see a lightning storm, ask for a sign or a psychic vision. Close your eyes and let any messages come to mind.

I take the action I need
to be where I need to be.

Self-assurance: Breathe like lightning!

Confidence comes like a bolt of lightning; sometimes it's unexpected, but often you can sense it building. Like any feeling, self-assurance can be conjured with a little help, some focused breathing, and lightning-inspired imagery.

1 Stand with feet hip-width apart and lengthen your spine.

2 As you breathe, imagine a sliver of lightning that flickers in your belly and grows brighter as you exhale.

3 For every breath you take, the lightning gets more powerful. It grows in size and length, and the flicker becomes a flash that travels up into your chest and out of your mouth as you release your breath.

4 Continue to breathe in this way for a minute.

5 Feel the lightning glow and let it fill you with passion and confidence.

Illumination: Light up the path

When you're struggling to see a way forward, switch up your mindset and illuminate your path. Imagine firing a bolt of lightning from the top of your head. It surges onward, lighting up the path you must take. In this instant, visualize the way forward. See it as a clear and gleaming runway lit by thousands of sparks of light. Know that you can easily overcome any obstacles and see your way ahead.

Focus: Tell it like a story

Cut through the darkness, like lightning, to maintain your focus.

Bring a problem or difficult situation to mind and instead of trying to make sense of it, let it hang there. Don't force thoughts or ideas, simply weigh it up, as if you were looking at a portrait or a story from a distance. To help, draw a picture that sums up the situation, then use it as a storytelling prompt.

Look at the image and write a few sentences to describe what is happening. Now imagine you're going to create an ending for the story, a solution to the problem. It doesn't have to make sense; you can be creative with this. Just draw and describe what comes to mind.

Now try to come up with a different ending and picture. Keep repeating this process until you have at least three different conclusions. Look at the overall picture and ask yourself if any of the solutions you've drawn feel right. Perhaps one instantly stands out, or maybe the pictures trigger a new idea. Being objective in this way to get to the heart of the problem can restore your focus and provide clarity.

MEDITATION

Use this uplifting visualization to inspire and energize.

Imagine watching a storm in the distance. You can see the dazzling light show in the sky, the beautiful colors and threads of brightness that cut through the darkness. The air is fizzing with energy, and you can feel a sense of anticipation. It's as if the universe is putting on a show just for you. As you stand, you draw a deep breath in through your feet and then release it. You can feel your heart beating within your chest, and there's a flutter of excitement in your stomach. Your skin prickles and you feel ready to take on the world. You continue to watch the golden hues blazing through the sky. Breathe, draw in the energy, and know that this is your time to shine.

Journaling inspiration

- What makes you feel confident? Is it doing something you love, or maybe being with certain people?

- Consider your day—were there any moments when you felt truly powerful and in control? What helped you feel this way?

- Think of three things that you could do to build self-confidence, and write them down.

Fox

Resourcefulness • Exploration • Self-esteem • Courage

With its vibrant red coat, sharp pointy ears, and a snout ready to sniff out mischief, it's no wonder the fox has a reputation for being "foxy." From the city dwellers who scavenge a living from dumpsters and trash bins to country foxes hunting and stealing for survival, they all use their wits to survive. Beautifully bold and daringly brave, the humble fox has attitude.

This is an instinctual creature, prepared to go out on a limb and embrace the unknown. Tapping into the fox's blessings can help you to become more resourceful and flexible. You'll discover the joy of being spontaneous and learn that stepping out of your comfort zone can bring untold gifts while also boosting self-esteem.

Your daily intention

"Today I will be like a curious fox; I will live by my wits, engage my ingenuity, and be ready to embark on new adventures."

Use the morning mantra with a quick creative exercise to ignite the imagination.

1 Imagine you could create the perfect day. What would happen? Perhaps you'd meet someone special, or maybe you'd get to be boss for the day. Whatever you'd choose, imagine right now that this is going to happen. See it like a film of the day ahead and run through it in your mind.

2 When you've finished, think of one word to sum up how you felt during the visualization—for example, "happy" or "excited."

3 Repeat the morning mantra, and at the end say "I am happy/excited," or whichever word you picked: "Today I will be like a curious fox; I will live by my wits, engage my ingenuity, and be ready to embark on new adventures. I am..."

Fox folklore

The fox is known for its quick wit and mercurial ways. A wily trickster worldwide, this cunning character knows how to outsmart even the sharpest opponent, but do not underestimate the spiritual significance of this creature. In mythology the fox is gifted with a number of powers, from stealing the fire from the sun, to shifting shape at the twitch of a tail.

The Celts believed the fox was a master of disguise, able to switch from human to animal. The Native Americans recognized the animal as a charlatan but also a positive omen. They honored the resourceful ways of the fox. In contrast, the Japanese were not so enthralled, believing foxes were evil shapeshifting beings called Kitsune. Mostly female, they were stunningly beautiful in human form but known for their deceitful ways.

Folklore fix

Create a fox charm for good fortune. Take a piece of amber, which is associated with fox energy, and pop it in a red charm bag. Keep the charm about your person to draw luck.

Self-esteem: Revel in your victories

The fearless fox rarely doubts its ability to survive and thrive, and uses every moment to excel. Do the same by remembering your awesomeness!

Bring to mind a moment when you felt on top of the world, a time when you overcame an obstacle or managed to achieve a goal against the odds. Run through the memory in your head, as if you're living it again. Enjoy the emotions associated with it. Now run through the memory once more, but this time as if it's in slow motion.

Engage your senses as you do this and take in as much of the experience as you can. Ask yourself why this particular memory makes you feel good. Reminding yourself of victories, big and small, boosts self-esteem and helps you realize your talents.

Resourcefulness: Sort your den

A quick-thinking fox uses what's within reach to make the most of every opportunity. You can do the same, by paying attention to your belongings, identifying what is useful, and clearing the clutter.

1 Start with one room and assess what you can see and what is tucked away.

2 Look at every item and ask yourself, do I really need or want this? Does it still serve a purpose?

3 If it doesn't, consider how you might upcycle it or use it in a different way. For example, you can revamp a cushion or re-cover it, or turn it into a pet bed.

4 Be inventive and challenge yourself to come up with alternative ideas for the belongings you really want to keep but don't use anymore.

Recycling and upcycling can help you see the potential in everything and develop a resourceful attitude.

Courage: Go red!

Foxes come in different shades, but the red fox is known for its boldness, and no wonder, sporting such a vibrant hue! The next time you need to bolster your courage, wear something red. From a full-on bright red outfit, to a splash of red lipstick or an striking scarf, let this eye-catching color build you up!

MEDITATION

Experience the exhilaration of running alongside the fox with this uplifting visualization.

Imagine that you're walking down a country path. You don't know where you're going, and you're taking your time, enjoying the warm sun on your face. Ahead you see a flicker of movement, something that catches your eye. You pick up speed, and as you follow the curve in the path, you see what caught your attention: a beautiful red fox standing in your way. For a second your eyes meet in silent understanding, then the fox is off. You follow, jogging lightly to keep up with your furry friend, and soon you are entering a patch of woodland, dense and full of mystery. You breathe in the power of the place as you move through the trees. The fox leads you into the heart of the wood, until eventually you lose sight of your guide. Take a moment to enjoy the adventure. Breathe and relax.

Exploration: Try something new

The curious fox is not afraid to go off track on the hunt for new experiences. Whether venturing into fresh territory or having a rummage in a different bin, the fox knows it's always worth broadening your horizons.

Be adventurous in your creative pursuits and let fox lead you up a new path. If there's something you've always wanted to try, then try it. You don't have to excel at your chosen pastime, as long as you enjoy it and take something from the experience.

If you've always wanted to paint, invest in some watercolors, look outside your window, and let the landscape inspire you. Do you daydream about turning your hand to pottery? Make today the day you sign up for that class.

Struggling to think of something new? Make a list of all the things you enjoy doing. This will help you identify areas to explore.

*Every moment is an opportunity to grow
and experience new adventures.*

Journaling inspiration

- What adventures have you had today? Small ones count, so include simple things such as trying out a new recipe or taking a different route home.
- Consider each adventure and how it made you feel. What did you enjoy? What were you nervous about?
- List the ways that you could be more adventurous in your life.

Star

Community • Self-worth
Energy • Abundance

The twinkling stars we see in the sky are really balls of gas that give off immense energy. Fiery hot and packed with potential, they shine with a power that is hard to ignore. They are a symbol of light, a divine blessing from the celestial realms, and a glimpse of the unknown. They hint at wonders to come and offer hope in its purest form.

You, too, can be imbued with this magical energy, by embracing star power and taking it to your heart. Just like the stars, you have the ability to shine, even on the darkest of nights. You can step into your personal power, invite hope and abundance into your life, and nurture your sparkle, by tapping into this cosmic blessing.

Your daily intention

"Today I will be a shining star: I will unleash my sparkle and bring light and power to the darkness."

Set your intention for the day by combining the morning mantra with a magical shower experience.

1 Stand beneath the shower and close your eyes.

2 As you wash, imagine that you're coating your body in glittery stardust.

3 Work from head to toe and massage your skin lightly.

4 Feel the stardust being absorbed as you cleanse.

5 Feel your body sparkle under the flow of water.

6 Take a deep breath in, and as you exhale say your morning mantra, with feeling:
"Today I will be a shining star: I will unleash my sparkle and bring light and power to the darkness."

Star folklore

In cultures around the world, stars represent divine guidance and protection. From their appearance in the heavens to the way they shine their light upon us, it's no surprise the ancients believed they had magical significance. Stargazing was a way to divine the future. Omens such as a shooting star were held in high regard. From making a wish, to the belief that each star represented a soul making its journey to the next life, stars were seen as symbols of hope and light.

Often, they were associated with deities, and the constellations, which are groups of stars, were given mythical names and status. Ancient Greek and Roman astronomers believed that popular legends were played out in the celestial realm for all to witness.

Abundance: See the bigger picture

The night sky is vast and littered with stars. While these stars might appear to stand alone, they are interconnected and part of a much bigger, bountiful galaxy and, beyond that, the universe. Tap into the abundance of the universe by expanding your awareness of where you are in the world right now.

Take a deep breath in, and as you exhale, take your awareness outside of your body. Imagine you're looking down on yourself and the surrounding area. Each time you inhale, imagine you're traveling further away. Take your consciousness outside of where you are, the room or building you might be in, up into the sky, and then even further. Imagine you're a shining star looking down upon the earth. See the beauty all around you and know that you are connected to every living thing. Notice how rich this makes you feel. Everything you want is within your grasp; all you have to do is ask the universe, then trust in the flow of abundance.

Folklore fix

Write your dearest wish on a piece of paper and place it in an envelope along with the Star card from a tarot deck. Seal it and make your wish silently while gazing up at the night sky. Leave the envelope on a window ledge overnight, and in the morning retrieve the card and replace it in the deck.

Community: Create a network of stars

Hope is contagious. It spreads from person to person. With a few encouraging words, a smile, or something much deeper, you can lift the spirits and create a sense of community in the process.

1 Consider the people in your life who make you feel good. Why is this? Perhaps they're fun, able to see the lighter side of things, or maybe they care and listen to what you have to say.

2 Each one is a star in your life, and it doesn't matter where they are, you are connected to them by a thread of light. Picture this in your mind, like a giant constellation.

3 Whenever you need to feel connected, bring to mind all the stars that make up your circle, and remember that you play your part in the community, too.

Energy: Let your star shine

Imagine a star in the center of your chest, sparkling with energy and power. Now picture it getting bigger and brighter with every breath that you take, until it fills your chest. Imagine the light seeping out through your skin. See this brightness extending in every direction. Feel the power of your presence grow as the star takes over your body and connects with your soul.

Self-worth: Tap into your inner star

Draw a large five-pointed star on a piece of paper. In the center write your name. Along each of the points write something positive about yourself. This could be something that you like about your appearance or your personality, or it could be a talent or characteristic.

Now imagine that this star, which lists five fantastic things about you, is hovering above your head for the rest of the day. Wherever you go, whoever you're with, the star is there. All you have to do to access its power is to bring the diagram to mind and recall the five amazing things about yourself.

The good news is that you can have more than one star. You can have an entire constellation of stars hovering above you—there is no limit. All you have to do is draw the extra stars and think of more positive things to say about yourself.

This esteem-boosting exercise helps you to appreciate who you are and what gives you star quality.

> *When I am true to myself, my light shines even brighter.*

MEDITATION

Find inner peace with this relaxing visualization.

Imagine you are sitting beneath a blanket of stars. The air is warm and sweet, and you feel the gentle kiss of a breeze touch your cheek. You lie back on the grass and feel the earth support you as you stare up at the heavenly realms. Inky black, the velvet sky sweeps down to greet you, and you let out a sigh of relief. All is well in your world. You are here, experiencing this moment of serenity. As you look at the stars, you notice patterns forming, shapes that blend into one. You feel connected to the universe, a part of a much greater picture. You exhale and feel every part of your body relax.

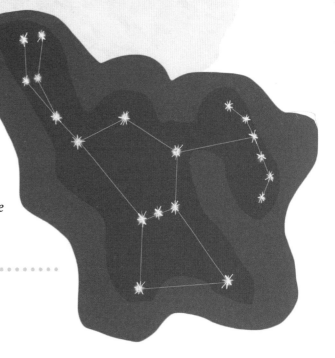

Journaling inspiration

- Think of your day, and pick out the moments when you felt truly hopeful. What made you feel that way?

- If you can't identify any moments of hope, consider why.

- What fills you with hope? Perhaps it's something simple like a rainbow or a glorious sunrise, or spending time with your favorite people.

- Write a list of things that you could do daily to renew your sense of hope.

Snake

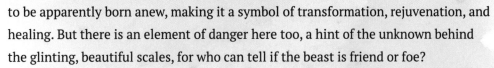

**Regeneration • Healing
Renewal • Bravery**

Moving low and lithe, with little sound, the
snake is a creature of mystery. It sheds its skin
to be apparently born anew, making it a symbol of transformation, rejuvenation, and
healing. But there is an element of danger here too, a hint of the unknown behind
the glinting, beautiful scales, for who can tell if the beast is friend or foe?

When you connect with the snake, you enter a world of transformation. Moving
from one state of being to another, you find your true self and emerge recharged
and ready to take on the world. The snake can heal and rejuvenate, but only if you're
prepared to shed your skin and the things you no longer need.

Your daily intention

*"Today I shall be like the snake, moving forward with confidence in
an eternal dance of transformation and renewal."*

Combine movement, flexibility, and fun with the morning mantra to set
your daily intention.

1 The sinewy snake undulates to fill the space with its powerful presence. It moves
every part of its body in a fluid dance. Imagine for a couple of minutes that you
are going to be like a snake.

2 Stand on the spot, roll your shoulders back, and let your body ripple. There is no
order to this—the important thing is to move your body, flowing from one move
to the next.

3 Bend and sway from your waist, wiggle your hips, and flex each limb, creating
a gentle and flexible rhythm.

4 End by saying your mantra with confidence: "Today I shall be like the snake, moving
forward with confidence in an eternal dance of transformation and renewal."

Snake folklore

From ominous portents to fire-breathing serpents, snakes have featured in mythology since the dawn of time. Many cultures consider them evil; the slithering body and venomous bite might have something to do with this, and their ability to regenerate would have seemed like sorcery to the ancients.

In Norse mythology Jörmungandr was the powerful serpent, and son of the trickster god Loki, who grew in size to encircle the world. As such, he held everything in place, until the coming of Ragnarök, the world's destructive end.

To the Aztecs the snake was god-like in his guise as Quetzalcoatl, the god of wind, agriculture, and learning. He may have looked like a feathered rattlesnake, but this deity played a key role in the world's creation. In Buddhism, the mystical Naga, a race of half-human, half-cobra-like beings, were sent to protect the Buddha.

Healing: Generate healing energy

The snake is a symbol of healing because of its ability to regenerate. Take inspiration from this beautiful creature with some mindful healing.

Start by assessing your body right now. How do you feel—tired, stressed, full of energy? Take a deep breath and imagine that you're sending healing energy to wherever you need it the most. Now turn your attention to each body part and

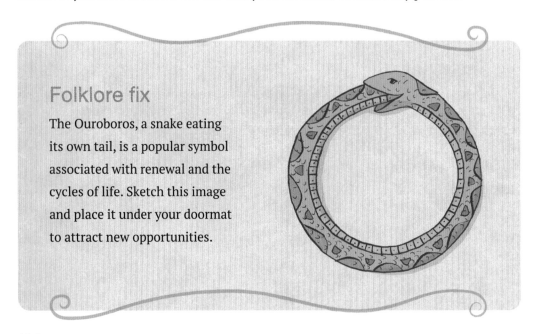

Folklore fix

The Ouroboros, a snake eating its own tail, is a popular symbol associated with renewal and the cycles of life. Sketch this image and place it under your doormat to attract new opportunities.

assess how it feels. Start at the top with your head, and work down your neck, spine, shoulders, arms, legs, and torso until you reach your feet. For each part, ask yourself how it truly feels. If there is discomfort there, ask yourself why, what could be causing it, and what you can do to prevent it. Then spend a few minutes breathing healing energy into this part. See the energy filling the space and soothing aches and pains.

Bravery: Breathing fire

Boost courage with this breathing exercise that you can do on the spot. Take inspiration from the fluid movement of the snake. Imagine that every breath you take moves like a fiery snake through your body. The flames ripple and spread, filling you with bravery. As you exhale, imagine expelling flames like a mythical serpent. Every breath imbues you with more power.

Renewal: Create a sacred circle

The snake is a cyclical creature. It moves in a constant loop, shedding and regenerating that which it no longer needs.

You are going to create a circle of renewal in your home from which you can meditate and access the power of rebirth. Create a sacred circle by positioning crystals, beads, or stones around a central point (or place a circular mat to mark the spot, if you like). Make this a sacred space by adding things that are important to you. For example you might want to build a small altar on a coffee table, with candles, flowers, and crystals, or just position some pictures and quotations that inspire you.

Sit in the center of the circle and contemplate renewal and what it means to you. Think of those times in your life when you came full circle. Perhaps you went through a difficult time and emerged the other side, stronger and re-energized. Even small cycles of renewal count, such as finishing a project at work. Acknowledge the power of renewal in your life and be open to its flow.

MEDITATION

Use this simple visualization to recharge and feel a sense of security.

Imagine you are surrounded by a circle of fire. You stand at the center, totally protected by the flames. You feel strong and secure. As you breathe you notice that the flames are moving, transforming into something more solid. The circle begins to spin slowly, and the sparks join together to form a giant snake-like creature. You watch as it encircles you, keeping negative energy at bay and allowing you the space to recharge. You feel a bond with this creature, as if you are one and the same. There's the spark of a flame growing inside of you, and it reaches outward connecting you with the snake's vibrant energy. Breathe, relax, and enjoy the warmth this brings.

Regeneration: Shed your skin

Snakes constantly outgrow their skin. They shed it when it no longer fits, and this helps with their general health, allowing the removal of parasites. We also need to grow emotionally and spiritually and cast away the layers to feel rejuvenated. This exercise is best done after a bath or shower.

1 Stand in the bathtub and use a body brush to eliminate toxins and shed negative energy. Start at the top by brushing from your shoulders along your arms, and work down your body.

2 As you do this, imagine that you're shedding a thin layer of negative energy. Picture it falling down the drain.

3 Use brisk movements to dislodge any energy blocks.

4 When you've finished, turn on the faucets and flush it away.

Every moment is a chance to start anew.

Journaling inspiration

- Consider what rejuvenates you. What puts a spring in your step, and a smile on your face?

- Think of three things you could do daily to help you feel rejuvenated. These could be self-care practices, or fun things that you enjoy.

- On a larger scale, is there something that you might need to let go of, to give you a sense of renewal? Write this down.

CHAPTER 4

The Element of Water

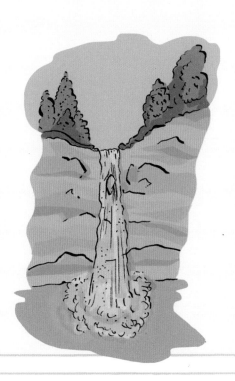

Water

The elixir of life, water replenishes and sustains. It soothes, refreshes, and washes away the things we no longer need. It adds vibrancy and color to whatever it touches, giving the kiss of life to a parched landscape and transforming it into a masterpiece. Water serves us, but it also works against us sometimes. Its power should not be underestimated, for while you might think water is all about the emotions, there is a resilience to this element, an urgency which cannot be ignored.

We all enjoy the benefits of water, but the creatures that make it their home, that inhabit and play within streams and rivers, know that it is a conduit of truth. Water is for the most part transparent, and can help us be honest and find the clarity we seek. Simply watching the ripples on the surface of a pond can teach us an important lesson, that for every thought and action, there is a reaction which creates a pattern.

Water is calming and has the ability to soothe a troubled mind. It cleans and heals, and—when it is free-flowing, like the ocean—cannot be stopped. It moves where it needs to be and can teach us to do the same.

The blessings and rituals in this section will help you move forward and release the past. You'll learn how to express yourself and go with the flow, open your heart, and also trust your intuition. Inspiration comes in many shapes and forms, and it is fluid and far-reaching, like this element. Connecting with the gifts of nature associated with the element of Water will soothe your soul and bring enlightenment.

WATER ACTIVITIES

To help you connect with this element, try to incorporate some of these activities into your schedule.

- Walk along the edge of a stream
- Visit the ocean and stroll through the gentle waves as they lap against the shore
- Take a refreshing shower
- Soak in the bathtub
- Make a wish and drop a penny into a well
- Take a bracing walk in the rain
- Stand in the presence of a large body of water, such as a lake, fast-flowing river, or beautiful waterfall
- Sip a glass of water

Moon

**Intuition • Enlightenment
Imagination • Inner peace**

The light of the moon is tender and soothing.
It enhances and illuminates, rather than stealing the show.
Gently, as the moon moves through each phase, it changes,
waxing and waning to mark the transitions, shifting shape, and
disappearing from view. Yet it is always present, even though we
cannot see it. There is a sense of wonder about this magical orb, a presence that
hints at the unknown.

Like the moon, you also move through transitions during your day, whether
physically as energy levels dip and soar, emotionally to match your moods, or
spiritually. Connecting with the moon can help you ride these changes with ease,
shed light on areas of your life that need cleansing, and boost your intuitive powers.

Your daily intention

*"Today I shall be like the magical moon, a shining jewel in the night sky.
I will unleash my translucent light and illuminate all dark spaces."*

Set your intention for the day by infusing your aura with the moon's vibrant light.

1 Stand with your shoulders back and your feet hip-width apart.

2 Close your eyes and visualize the moon in the sky. Imagine you're bathed
   in its luminescence.

3 Take a long breath in and draw it along your spine and over your head in a loop.

4 Repeat the breath, and as you draw it over your body, imagine it's a thread
   of white light.

5 Continue to do this for three more breaths, then open your eyes and give your
   body a shake.

6 Say the mantra out loud: "Today I shall be like the magical moon, a shining jewel in the night sky. I will unleash my translucent light and illuminate all dark spaces."

Moon folklore

The moon features in folklore around the world. It is an object of fascination, a magical orb to be worshipped, and a tool for manifestation. Each moon phase is associated with a different kind of energy, and spells are cast depending on which phase is dominant. The waxing moon is the best time to attract new things and put plans in motion. The waning moon can help you release the past and break bad habits. The new moon conjures fresh starts and initiatives, while the full moon is the time to fulfill wishes and reap rewards.

Moon deities are popular in mythologies across the globe, and while most consider the moon to embody female energy, there are some male examples, such as the Mesopotamian moon god Nanna. In Greek mythology, Selene was the beautiful and powerful goddess of the moon.

Folklore fix

On the night of a full moon, make a wish for something you would like to attract into your life.

Inner peace: Journey to the moon

This mindful visualization should help to give you a moment of peace and distance you from stress.

Breathe deeply to calm your mind, then visualize the moon in the sky. Imagine it getting bigger and brighter with every breath that you take. Continue to focus on it expanding and drawing closer to you as you breathe in and out. Eventually it is so large that you can almost reach out and touch it. Drink in its beauty and feel its gentle presence. Take a deep breath in, and as you exhale, imagine the moon slowly reducing in size, moving further away until it is nothing more than a pinprick of light in the sky.

Enlightenment: Take a moon shower

Connect with the energy of the moon by taking a moon shower. This can be done during any phase, but for the best results, perform it on the evening of a full moon or when the moon is waxing.

1 Go outside or stand in front of a window with a clear view of the moon.

2 Spend a few minutes gazing at the moon. Let any thoughts flow into your head, but instead of focusing on them, bring your attention back to the view.

3 Imagine a river of energy flowing from the moon, and allow it to bathe you in vibrant white light. It sweeps over your body, cleansing and illuminating every part.

4 Breathe, relax, and enjoy feeling refreshed and enlightened.

Imagination: Moon musing

The moon has inspired poets and artists for centuries, so let it provide you with inspiration at any point during your day.

Stop and bring the moon to mind. Think of three words that you associate with it, for example, "magical," "bright," and "light." Now have a go at putting these words into an affirmation that you can use right now to trigger your imagination. You might say, "I am *magical* like the moon; my inner *light* shines *bright*."

I let my intuition be my guide
in all things.

Intuition: Turn on your inner light

Turn the moon's light inward to ignite your intuition.

Take a moment to focus on the space behind your eyes. Imagine falling back into your head and looking outward. All you can see is a white circular screen, a blank canvas without any pictures. Breathe deeply and turn up the light on the screen. Slowly an image of the moon appears. As you continue to look, you can see patterns and images appearing on its surface. You might see shapes, words, or even pictures. Random thoughts may pop into your mind. Simply observe, as if you are watching a film at the cinema. When you're ready, flip the screen off and return to the real world. Note down anything you can remember, as it could prove useful in the future.

When you cast light on your intuition and allow yourself the time and space to simply be, psychic insights emerge.

MEDITATION

Use this soothing meditation to release stress and relax before bed.

Close your eyes and imagine you are lying beneath a blanket of stars. The sky is dark, but there's a glow emanating from the moon. You gaze up at it and feel the light hit the top of your head. As you exhale, the light travels over your body. You can feel this shimmering energy sweeping through you, clearing away any negativity that has collected during your day. As you inhale, you are cocooned in healing energy, wrapped in a cloak of whiteness that cushions every part of your body. You feel light as a feather, as if you could rise up into the air and float into space.

Journaling inspiration

- Consider your day and pick out a meaningful moment. Perhaps you shared some words of comfort with a colleague, or simply found a moment of peace amid the activity. Focus on this moment and what it meant to you, then give thanks for it.

- Identify three things that help you find inner peace.

Fish

Flow • Grace • Learning • Gratitude

Whether swimming in a school or taking a solo dip, the fish makes it all look effortless. With elegance, it weaves a watery path toward its destination. Does it know where it's going? Perhaps, but the most important thing is to be fluid, to let life lead the way on a tantalizing journey. The lissome fish has learned the lessons of the past and moves toward the future with grace.

You can do the same, by letting go. Take your inspiration from this blessing, be supple and subtle in your approach. A light touch and an open heart can bring delightful twists and turns and provide the opportunity to expand your knowledge.

Your daily intention

"Today I will be like a fish, elegant and agile; I will swim upstream and let the glistening waters soothe my soul."

Combine the morning mantra with a gentle exercise to set your intention.

1 Lie on your back on a hard surface. Relax and let your body sink into the floor.

2 Take a deep breath in and say your mantra aloud: "Today I will be like a fish, elegant and agile; I will swim upstream and let the glistening waters soothe my soul."

3 As you exhale, gently bend your legs and bring them in to your body.

4 Wrap your arms around your knees and allow yourself to rock. Let the momentum of your body carry you forward and back.

5 After a minute, slowly extend your legs, relax, and return to your original position.

6 Repeat the mantra once more.

Fish folklore

Fish have long been associated with the unknown. They live beneath the surface in a watery realm, which is normally unseen by the human eye. Within this kingdom of secrets, they derive sacred knowledge, which makes them synonymous with wisdom. The Celts, in particular, associated fish with otherworldly intelligence. The salmon was most prized for its wisdom, which it gained from eating hazelnuts from the Well of Knowledge.

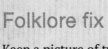

Folklore fix

Keep a picture of two fish together in your pocket to increase the flow of love in your life and cement a new relationship.

In eastern India, the fish was a symbol of transformation and creation—in one myth the god Vishnu changes into a fish, to save the world from a devastating flood. In China, fish ornaments and charms are given as wedding gifts, to represent unity and love. In magic, the fish is often linked to goddesses and feminine energy and is associated with the ability to go with the flow.

Learning: Be more fish

Bring to mind a moment when you felt you were "in the flow," or when everything seemed to fall into place at the right time.

Run through the memory in your mind. Relive the experience by engaging with the emotions you felt. See it like a film that you are now a part of. Every time your mind begins to wander, bring it back to the start of the memory, breathe, and begin the journey again.

When you reach the end, notice how you feel. Consider what you learned from the experience and if anything else comes to mind having run through the memory again. When we reflect on events, we tend to see more than we did at the time of experiencing them. Think of one lesson that you can draw upon in the future.

*Every moment is an opportunity to give thanks
for the gifts I've been given.*

Gratitude: Say thank you for your blessings

Give thanks for all the wonderful things and people that swim into your life by
acknowledging them as you flow through the day.

- First thing in the morning, think of three things to be grateful for. You might give
  thanks for the rising sun, the gift of a new day, and your body, which allows you to
  move about and get on with things.
- At lunchtime do the same: find three things to be grateful for and give thanks.
- Finally, at the end of your day, pick another three things to add to your list and say
  thank you.
- Get into the habit of expressing gratitude; it lifts the spirits and attracts more of
  the same by raising your energy vibration.

Grace: Go with the tide

When things don't go your way, instead of fixating on them and creating more
negativity, accept them with good grace. Say "stop" in your mind and switch up your
emotions by focusing on something that has gone right. Recall what happened and
enjoy those happy feelings. Know that things can go for and against you in life.
Remember: fish don't swim against the tide, they go with it and glide with ease.

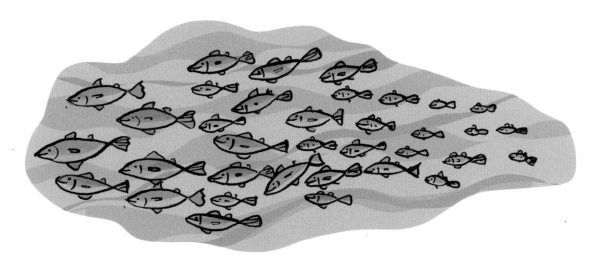

Flow: Dive in deep

Find a picture of the ocean that you like. Spend some time looking at it. Take in everything you can see and notice how it makes you feel. Make it real and imagine you're there, swimming in the icy water. What do you notice as you look around? Perhaps you pick out sea birds in flight, or a ship in the distance?

Now close your eyes and imagine that you've taken a dip under the sea. How different is the picture here? What can you see? What do you feel? Create an underwater scene in your mind. When you're ready, have a go at doing it on paper, by drawing, painting, or even describing the picture using words and poetry. Have fun with this and enjoy letting your creativity flow.

By reversing the picture and recreating it from a fresh perspective, you are being flexible. Practicing this skill in your creative pursuits will help you take a flexible approach in other areas of your life.

MEDITATION

Use this visualization to let go and enjoy being in the moment.

Imagine you're floating on a gentle river. You don't know where you are or where you're going, but it doesn't matter. You are happy, content with letting the water carry you forward. You close your eyes and concentrate on what you can feel: the trickle of water that tickles your skin and the embrace of the water that buoys your arms and legs. You can feel the fish beneath you; they too are going with the flow. You take a deep breath in and relax. You feel safe here, supported by the undercurrent. There is no pressure to do anything, no worries or fears. You can simply be yourself and let the gentle river take you on a journey of discovery.

Journaling inspiration

- Reflect on your day. What have you learned?

- Identify three things that you have discovered on your journey today.

- Did you meet any resistance? Why was this? It can be hard to be like a fish and go with the flow, but when you do, the current helps you along and you feel in sync with the universe.

Rain

Refreshment • Cleansing • Calm • Self-expression

An essential part of the cycle of life, rain is all things to all people. It nourishes and sustains. It cleanses the earth and adds a touch of magic, bringing color and depth to the landscape. There's a sense of calm after a sudden downpour, a feeling that the slate has been wiped clean. Rain purifies; it is a purging of emotions, a way to unburden and express yourself.

Working with this blessing will help you release pent-up feelings and unblock stagnant energy. You'll learn how to express yourself in a positive way and purify your mind and body, so that you feel refreshed and centered. Rain can help to wash things away, and also brighten and lighten the mood.

Your daily intention

"Today I will be like the rain; I will allow my emotions to flow freely and express myself with ease."

Use the morning mantra with this exercise to add color and glow to your day. Rain makes everything shine brighter, and a smile can do the same.

1 Stand in front of a mirror, think of something joyful, and smile.

2 Look at your face in detail. Notice the way this one expression changes your features, bringing them to life.

3 Notice the way your eyes sparkle and your face lights up as the joy reaches every part of you.

4 Breathe and say your morning mantra: "Today I will be like the rain; I will allow my emotions to flow freely and express myself with ease."

Rain folklore

As humans we rely on rain; it is life-giving and essential to new growth. However, too much can set us on a path of destruction, causing floods and damage to properties and livestock. It's no wonder the ancients believed rain was a gift of the gods. The changes in weather they experienced reflected the changing moods of the deities. If they were displeased, they could withhold rainfall, or send too much as punishment.

In China, it was thought that all weather types were controlled by dragons, with Yinglong, also known as the Responding Dragon, being the one who brought the rain. His enormous tail carved riverbeds into the earth, so that the rainwater could flow and gather. A generous entity, Yinglong could be petitioned by performing a rain-dragon dance or molding his form out of clay.

Folklore fix

Leave a bowl out to catch the rain, then use the rainwater to make ice cubes. Pop one in a handkerchief and roll it over your face for an instant beauty boost.

Calm: Experience the stillness

After rainfall, there's a stillness to the air, a sense of calm that you can bring into your own life when you need to regroup.

Stop, breathe, and center yourself by focusing on your core in the middle of your belly. Breathe in and tighten your muscles, then breathe out and relax. Imagine you're standing in the middle of a downpour, a sudden torrent of rain. Suddenly everything freezes. The rain, the movement around you, any thoughts or worries that have come to mind—everything stops. You cannot see or hear anything. You are caught within the moment, isolated and alone. All you can do is experience the stillness. If it helps, close your eyes and simply breathe. When you're ready, release the freeze and feel the rain fall around you. Hear the swooshing sound as it races past you and bring your attention back to your body. Slowly re-engage with your surroundings.

Refreshment: Feel the thrill of the chill

There's something refreshing about rainfall. After a shower, everything feels more animated and the colors of the landscape come to life. Harness this power for yourself using the element of Water.

1 During your morning shower, after you've cleansed, turn the temperature down. For 30 seconds make it as cold as you can bear it.

2 Turn your face upward and experience the icy abrasion as the water hits your face. Be sure to breathe slowly and deeply as you adjust to the cooler temperature.

3 Imagine that it's pure rainwater that is cleansing your aura, and that for every freezing drop, you feel more alive and vibrant.

4 Pat yourself dry and give your body a good shake to stimulate circulation. You should feel refreshed, energized, and ready for your day.

Cleansing: Let the rain quench you

Instead of shying away from a downpour, get the waterproofs on and venture outside, turn your face to the sky, and absorb the rain. Imagine that each drop is imbued with positive energy, which cleanses your body. Feel the rhythm of each trickle as it hits your head. Focus on the pattern and beat and enjoy the icy touch of each drop.

Self-expression: Let your ideas flow

Imagine that your ideas and thoughts are drops of rain cascading in a torrent from the sky. Give them the chance to fall by giving yourself free rein to daydream.

You'll need a piece of paper and a pen. Set a timer for five minutes, and make sure you won't be distracted. Take a couple of deep breaths to center yourself, then let your thoughts hit the paper. Don't edit, or try and make sense of what you write, simply let your pen do the talking. Even if it seems like gobbledygook, it doesn't matter. This is about letting your creativity flow. If you're struggling to write anything, just keep breathing and start with a word or a feeling. Write it down and see what happens next. Let your mind wander and describe what you see.

When the five minutes are up, read your musings. They might not make sense, but you could also be surprised by what you've written. This exercise can help you connect with your deepest feelings and also your subconscious mind.

*I follow my heart and express
my emotions clearly.*

MEDITATION

This calming meditation can be done as a visualization, or practice it for real on a rainy day.

Imagine you're sitting by a window, watching the rain come down. As the raindrops increase in size and volume you can see less of the outside world, so you shift your focus. You concentrate on what you can hear, the pitter patter as the rain hits the windowpane. It's a gentle, lilting rhythm that matches your breathing. Trace the path that each drop takes as it slowly trickles down the glass. Listen as the tapping sound picks up speed. Let it become a background rhythm as you drift into a deeper state of relaxation. If your mind starts to wander, bring it back to the pattern and melody of the raindrops. Let the rain soothe you into a calmer state of mind.

Journaling inspiration

- Reflect on your emotions throughout the day. Were there moments when you felt more in touch with your feelings than others? How did you express those emotions; did you hold them in, ignore them, or release them?

- Think of three ways that you could express how you feel in a positive way.

Otter

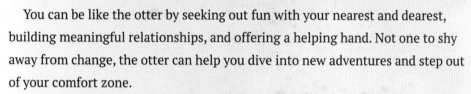

Playfulness • Adventure
Affection • Connection

Bristling with energy and a sense of adventure, the otter loves to explore. From underwater realms to the riverbank, there is so much to see and do and this playful character makes the most of every second. The otter loves having fun with friends and family: togetherness is important, and those impromptu opportunities to show you care are high on the list of an otter's favorite things.

You can be like the otter by seeking out fun with your nearest and dearest, building meaningful relationships, and offering a helping hand. Not one to shy away from change, the otter can help you dive into new adventures and step out of your comfort zone.

Your daily intention

"Today I shall be like a playful otter, making the most of every opportunity and seeking out new adventures."

Use the morning mantra with this exercise to put you in a positive mindset.

1 Sit on the edge of your bed and lengthen your spine.

2 Roll your shoulders back, lift your chin upwards, and take a breath. As you do, place your hands on your diaphragm and laugh.

3 Feel your body move as the sound reverberates.

4 Even if you don't feel the slightest bit amused, continue to laugh until you do!

5 Build up your laughter so that you're exaggerating it. Be loud and over the top. You should find that you're soon smiling with real joy.

6 Say the morning mantra with feeling: "Today I shall be like a playful otter, making the most of every opportunity and seeking out new adventures."

Otter folklore

The friendly otter is popular in most mythologies and renowned for its joyful behavior. As such, it was considered a positive omen and a symbol of happiness and love. The Celts revered otters, seeing them as helpful characters and calling them "water dogs." In one Irish tale, called The Voyage of Máel Dúin, otters from the Isle of Otter kept the sailors well fed by bringing them fresh salmon.

According to Scottish folklore, there once lived Otter Kings, who were accompanied by seven magical otters. If you were lucky to capture one of these otters you could claim a wish, but these slippery characters were invincible and extremely hard to pin down. In ancient Persia, otters were prized over all other creatures, and killing one was a punishable crime.

Folklore fix

Looking for love? Find an ornament or a picture of two otters together and place it on your bedside table.

Adventure: Expand your circle

Appreciate the joy that expansion brings with this mindful technique to instill a sense of adventure.

Start by focusing on your breathing, the rise and fall of your chest and the sound of each breath. Slow down your breathing and notice how this quietens your mind. Pay attention to your immediate environment. Imagine you are standing at the heart of a small circle. Notice everything that surrounds you; look at, listen to, smell, and taste everything within the space. Now extend the circle a little wider and take note of any changes—you might notice objects or people that weren't in your immediate circle of experience. Continue to widen the circle, to take in even more of the environment. What do you notice now? As you continue to widen the circle, your world becomes fuller, richer, and more engaging.

Affection: Get the hugging bug

Otters show affection by touching and playing, and sea otters even hold hands while sleeping. Show your affection to your nearest and dearest by giving more hugs.

- As you pull the person in for a cuddle, make a silent wish for love and imagine wrapping them up in a fluffy blanket. Feel the love traveling from your heart to theirs as you connect.

- It's also important to consider yourself and give out a little self-love with a hug. Cross over your arms, place your hands on your shoulders, and say "I love you!" Then relax and enjoy the feeling of warmth and security.

Connection: Share your smile

Otters love to connect with each other using gestures. They communicate through nose touching, head jerking, and high-pitched squeals. Improve your daily connections with a simple smile and a kind word. Whether you're with a coworker, friend, or stranger, the power of a smile is contagious. Look them in the eye, smile from the heart, and offer a word of encouragement. You'll notice the smile is reflected back and there's an instant meeting of minds when using these gestures.

Playfulness: Regress to childhood

Otters enjoy play. It doesn't matter how old they get—having fun puts a wiggle in their walk. Take inspiration from them, by going back to your youthful roots.

Think about your childhood and the things you enjoyed doing. What were your favorite games? Did you enjoy playing team games or were you happier going solo and using your imagination? Remember those pastimes you loved and make a list. Think of hobbies, too, things that you don't do anymore but enjoyed at the time. Once you have your list, go through and star the things that really brought you joy.

Look again at the list and at the items you've starred, and consider whether you'd like to try them again. You don't have to take them up properly, but sometimes just playing a game from childhood is enough to re-ignite your playful spirit.

You might find that once you try something, you'll want to do it regularly, or it might give you more ideas of things to try. Make a point of picking one thing from your list to try each month.

MEDITATION

Use this uplifting visualization to adopt a positive attitude.

You are sitting on some rocks by the beach. It is deserted, except for a handful of sea birds picking at shells by the shore. The sun is low in the sky and there is a gentle breeze. You can smell the saltiness of the sea in the air and hear the distant call of a gull in flight. As you sit motionless, you notice movement to your left, by a smaller group of rocks. You see two bodies entwined and rolling in damp sand. From the slick brown fur and round bright eyes, you realize that they are otters playing. You watch, amused by their antics. Their tiny squeals are carried on the wind, and you chuckle as they chase each other, oblivious to your presence. In this moment you feel relaxed, in love with life, and able to see the joy all around you.

I look for the positive in everything and allow my playful side to emerge.

Journaling inspiration

- What made you smile or laugh today?

- Were there any standout moments that brought you joy? Consider what was special about these moments.

- Could you introduce more play into your day?

- Think about the things you do out of work, and consider if you need to revamp your leisure time.

Sea

Mystery • Letting go • Personal power • Compassion

Bringing continents together and providing a channel of industry, the sea's importance is clear. It is nurturing, home to a variety of aquatic life, and a place of great wonder. Who knows what secrets are hidden within the briny deep? Explore though we might, we can never fully understand the power and might of the ocean. Ever flowing, ever present, the sea is both serene and wild, a force of nature that cannot be tamed.

You can be like the sea and connect with its energy by learning to let go and flow with the tides in your life. Let the waters of change release you from the past and plunge deep beneath the surface, to truly understand your fears, hopes, and dreams. The sea can help you discover hidden strengths and also heal your heart and mind.

Your daily intention

"Today I will be like the sea, a powerful force that ebbs and flows with grace and beauty."

Get your flow on with this exercise that combines the morning mantra with fluid stretches.

1 Stand with your feet wide apart and lengthen your spine.

2 Say your mantra aloud, then bend your knees, keeping your spine straight: "Today I will be like the sea, a powerful force that ebbs and flows with grace and beauty."

3 Extend your right arm out to the side in a wave motion, then return to your side.

4 Do the same with your left. Keep the movements as fluid as you can.

5 Now let both arms flow together to the front, then return to your sides.

6 Return to standing position and give your limbs a shake.

Sea folklore

Enigmatic and alluring, the sea has been a source of fascination since the beginning of time. With an underwater realm that could have sprung from the pages of a fantasy novel, it's easy to see how stories of the Lost City of Atlantis emerged. According to Greek legend, it sank underwater at the hands of the gods.

Creatures lurk within the deep, beasts such as the Nordic Kraken, a gigantic squid-like monster with enormous tentacles that ripped ships apart and dragged them

Folklore fix

Shells are the treasures of the sea. When you're next at the coast, take a walk along the beach and find a shell that you're drawn to. Whisper your deepest heartfelt wishes to the shell and keep it with you as a charm to attract your desires.

under. Then there were the Sirens of Greek legend, beguiling and beautiful but equally dangerous as they lured men with their sweet voices and killed them for pleasure. Mermaids too have a reputation for leading sailors to their doom, although some would calm the seas for those who won their favor. A place of mystery and enchantment, the sea symbolizes life, power, and creativity.

Mystery: Look beyond the surface

The sea is full of the unknown. You can never really be sure what's going on beneath the waves, and even when it appears calm, the depths harbor a myriad of secrets. Learn to look beyond the surface and recognize the mystery at work in your life, using the element of Water.

Take a dark bowl and half fill with warm water. Add a couple of drops of lavender oil to relax you. Place a towel over your head and gaze into the bowl. Let your eyes soften and inhale the sweet aroma. Let any patterns or images form on the surface of the water. Don't try and distinguish them, simply let them drift to the surface of your mind. Allow your thoughts to float in and out. Ask for an insight into your life and see what comes to mind.

Letting go: Water ceremony

Move forward and release the past with this watery ritual. If it's possible, find some free-flowing water in nature, or if you can make it to the ocean, even better. If not, you can do this ritual with some water in the bathtub.

1 Spend some time thinking about what you'd like to eliminate from your life. Perhaps you want to release the past, or let go of a negative pattern of thought or a bad habit.

2 Take a white flower to symbolize what you need to release and gently drop it in the water. As you do this, take a deep breath in and out, and feel yourself letting go.

3 Say, "I release you. I am free to move forward and be me."

*I relinquish my grip on the past and float
with joy into the future.*

Personal power: Cool down and power up

You can connect with the sea simply by drinking more water. You'll improve your hydration and also feel rejuvenated. Pour yourself a glass of chilled water, add a couple of ice cubes, and sip slowly. Visualize the icy water infusing every part of your body with strength and power.

Compassion: Draw out your compassion

The sea is nurturing and compassionate; it sustains and provides freely. Tap into these qualities with a creative exercise.

If compassion was a drawing, what would it be? A heart? A flower? A beautiful fish swimming in the sea? Perhaps it would be a design like a mandala, made up of ripples and waves. If you had to represent the feeling in an image, what would you use?

Think about what compassion means to you and bring to mind any moments of compassion that you have felt or experienced. Put pen to paper and let your creativity flow like the ocean. It doesn't matter what you draw, it's about tuning into that feeling. Use your imagination and daydream a little. If you're not feeling artistic, make the picture a collage and collect together images from magazines. When you've finished, position your creation somewhere that you can see it every day as a reminder to be more compassionate.

MEDITATION

This visualization will help you tap into the tranquil energy of the sea.

Imagine you're floating in the sea. Your entire body is relaxed, and your eyes are closed. You can feel the waves gently lapping against your skin. You feel cradled by the water, as if you are being held tight and supported. The sun kisses your skin, and you feel as though you could drift away into dream. In the distance you can hear sea birds calling, and the sound of children playing on the beach, but it is so far away. Right now, it is just you and the ocean, together in perfect harmony. You smooth your hands across the ripples, and feel the water slip between your fingers. You bob and weave in a rhythmic flow. You drink in the peace of this moment and let it calm your mind.

Journaling inspiration

- How easy do you find it to go with the flow? Do you find yourself resisting change? What happens when you stop fighting and live in the moment?
- Pick out moments in life when you feel you've been fluid like the sea, and remember how it felt.
- Highlight three things that would help you adopt a flexible attitude.

Waterfall

Release • Rejuvenation
Clarity • Purity

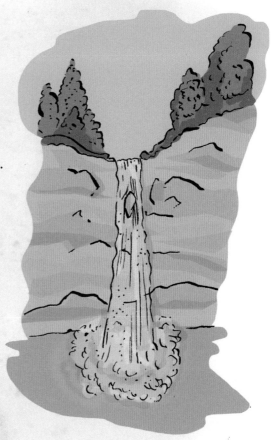

With crystal-clear waters that fall continuously, carving a path into the mountain, the waterfall is a never-ending force of nature. It soothes and purifies, bringing clarity, release, and rejuvenation. It is a joy to behold, and standing in the presence of such a blessing can induce calm emotions. It doesn't matter if the waterfall is a tumbling cascade or a freshwater trickle; it is a thing of beauty and sustenance.

Connecting with this blessing will help you release the past and find your own path by being flexible in the face of obstacles. You'll learn the power of purification and how cleansing the body and mind can revitalize your life and help you move forward with renewed focus.

Your daily intention

"Today I will be like a refreshing waterfall cascading down the mountainside. I will sparkle and flow with grace as I move toward my destination."

Use the morning mantra with this simple stretching exercise to set your intention for the day ahead.

1 Stand with your feet hip-width apart, and shoulders back and relaxed.

2 Take a deep breath in and roll your shoulders forward.

3 Slowly begin to bend from the waist, while letting your arms fall toward the floor.

4 Relax into the bend more and let your hands point downward.

5 Wiggle your fingers and extend the stretch until you feel a gentle pull along your arms and spine.

6 Release your breath and slowly return to a standing position.

7 State your mantra aloud: "Today I will be like a refreshing waterfall cascading down the mountainside. I will sparkle and flow with grace as I move toward my destination."

Waterfall folklore

It's no wonder waterfalls are such visions of beauty. Believed to be the bathing place of the gods, the waters held within are sacred and life-giving, blessed with the ability to transform those who are lucky enough to stand beneath the flow. In Hinduism, the waterfall is the stream of consciousness sent from the deities and offers light, abundance, and healing. It falls down from the celestial realms into the rivers and streams, where the great god Shiva resides.

In Norse mythology, the waterfall is a magical place, where you might find fairy folk lurking, something which is true throughout Scandinavia. One of the tallest falls in Iceland, known as Haifoss, is thought to be home to a giant ogress, who guards the river from unwanted visitors. In southern Iceland you'll find Skogafoss, a beautiful waterfall which, according to legend, hides an enormous chest of treasure.

Folklore fix

Stir a couple of drops of tea tree essential oil into a pitcher of warm water. Bend your head over the sink and use the scented water to rinse your hair. As the water flows, wish for purity of mind and body.

Rejuvenation: Energy streaming

For instant rejuvenation, imagine you're standing beneath a waterfall. The streams of water glisten like white shards, garlands of light that fall on the top of your head. The water surges through your scalp, down behind your eyes, into your neck, shoulders, and arms. It snakes along your spine, filling your chest and stomach, and filtering down into your pelvis, your thighs, and your calves, finally reaching your feet.

Here the streams burst from each sole into the ground, anchoring you in place. This waterfall of energy moves in a continual loop, connecting you to the heavens and the earth, and filling you with life force. Breathe and enjoy the sweeping sensation as the energy moves within you.

Clarity: Spring clean your head

Feeling muddled? Carry out this simple visualization,. which uses the cleansing power of the waterfall for clarity and focus.

Imagine that you're standing before a glorious waterfall that flows into a river. You stand at the water's edge, watching the gushing spray of water fall and twinkle in the sunlight. You peer into the frothy depths. The water is almost transparent and the surface shimmers. You breathe deeply and let images form before your eyes. You might see shapes, patterns, words, or pictures. Just let them stream before you and watch as they run their course along the river. Imagine that with every breath you are taking in the cleansing energy of the waterfall. After a few minutes, your mind should feel clearer. Make a note of any images that stay with you, as they may show you the way forward.

Release: Flush it away

Release the stress in your life by dipping into the flow. Turn on the cold faucet and imagine that it's a mini waterfall imbued with life-giving energy. Hold your wrists in the gushing water for 30 seconds. Close your eyes. Breathe, and feel the negative energy slipping down the drain. Whatever has been bothering you, let it go into the flow.

*With every breath, I release negative energy
and cleanse body and mind.*

Purity: Reflect and reconnect

Find a photograph of a waterfall and spend some time gazing at the image. Give yourself five minutes to write a paragraph about the picture.

Now look at the photograph again and consider how it makes you feel. Transport yourself to this place and imagine what it would be like to sit there and take it all in. What do you think you would hear, smell, taste? Engage all your senses and make the experience as real as possible. When you're ready, give yourself another five minutes to reflect on the waterfall and write another paragraph.

Compare the two. The first is your initial response to the picture, and while it might be descriptive, it is likely to be logical too. The second is more reflective and creative because you connected with the waterfall at a deeper, purer level.

Whenever you need to connect with the purity of one of nature's blessings, try this exercise to help you engage at a deeper level.

MEDITATION

Use this meditation to lull you to sleep. If you can find some background sounds of water flowing, it will help you relax.

Imagine you're standing at the top of a mountain, looking down on a waterfall. You watch the gentle trickles of water, winding and weaving down the mountainside. You mark each stage of their journey with your eyes, slowly breathing in time with the gentle stream. You marvel at the way these glistening tendrils make the rocky landscape come to life. You think of your own journey, how you flow through each day, making your way in the world. Your breath grows slower, deeper, as your chest rises and then falls, and you continue to watch the never-ending flux of the waterfall. Feel the fluid rhythm of your heart and the sound of your breath as you exhale.

Journaling inspiration

- Consider what obstacles you faced today. Perhaps you encountered problems, dilemmas, or just difficult people. How did you deal with it? Could you have been more fluid in your approach? Did you surge forward, or move around the things that were blocking you?

- Write down your thoughts as you reflect upon this subject.

INDEX